AN ILLNESS OBSERVED
THROUGH RELUCTANT EYES

AN ILLNESS OBSERVED
THROUGH
RELUCTANT
EYES

Encouragement, Ideas and Anecdotes
for Individuals Facing a Serious Illness
as a Patient or Caregiver

LISA PENCE

NASHVILLE

NEW YORK • LONDON • MELBOURNE • VANCOUVER

An Illness Observed Through Reluctant Eyes
Encouragement, Ideas and Anecdotes for Individuals
Facing a Serious Illness as a Patient or Caregiver

© 2019 LISA PENCE

Published in New York, New York, by Morgan James Publishing. Morgan James is a trademark of Morgan James, LLC. www.MorganJamesPublishing.com

The Morgan James Speakers Group can bring authors to your live event. For more information or to book an event visit The Morgan James Speakers Group at www.TheMorganJamesSpeakersGroup.com.

ISBN 978-1-64279-013-9 paperback
ISBN 978-1-64279-014-6 eBook
Library of Congress Control Number: 2018936340

Cover Design by:
Rachel Lopez
www.r2cdesign.com

Interior Design by:
Bonnie Bushman
The Whole Caboodle Graphic Design

In an effort to support local communities, raise awareness and funds, Morgan James Publishing donates a percentage of all book sales for the life of each book to Habitat for Humanity Peninsula and Greater Williamsburg.

Get involved today! Visit
www.MorganJamesBuilds.com

DEDICATION

CONTENTS

INTRODUCTION

In 2012, at age forty-eight, my husband Randy became seriously ill with myelofibrosis and underwent a bone marrow/stem cell transplant. Thrown into the middle of this illness we had never encountered before, I had no way of knowing what lie ahead. I searched for answers to questions I didn't even know to ask. How I would have appreciated a book with some suggestions for me as a caregiver and for my husband as a patient, concerning the path that lay before us! I wanted a true assessment. What was about to happen? Would we be able to persevere? I needed insight.

A book written from a similar experience was nowhere to be found. I attended caregiver workshops offered at the bone marrow clinic which helped, but I needed real-life, first-hand accounts, warts and all. I read blogs, but nothing gave me the whole story of a serious illness. I wanted real scenarios with real outcomes and information to help along the way, not a pretty picture for my benefit.

Since I couldn't find such a book, I decided to write one myself. If you're looking for real suggestions to real situations, this book is for you. Every illness has its own set of unique characteristics, symptoms, and outcomes, because none of us are alike. I know my experiences will not be exactly the same as yours, but my hope is you can apply some of the suggestions and encouragement in this book to your situation.

Whether you are about to become a caregiver or have been one for some time, whether you are a newly-diagnosed patient or have been fighting the good fight for months, I hope this book will help prepare you and offer you some comfort to know you are not alone. My prayer is that you may approach this path a stronger person, confident in the way for your journey ahead.

SOMETHING'S WRONG

I didn't know what was wrong, but something in the pit of my stomach told me something was not right. The little changes were not enough to snap us into action, however. It took multiple physical and behavioral differences happening simultaneously to awaken us to realization that everything was not as it should be.

My forty-eight-year-old husband, Randy, came into our house after work, walked up the stairs, and lay down on our bed. I have known Randy since we were fourteen-year-old middle schoolers, and throughout all our years together he always worked. In high school, he mowed lawns and cleared snow for several widows in our church and he held down two part-time jobs while attending full-time college. He rarely had free time.

The pace continued after we married. Randy managed an independent Christian bookstore in an outdoor strip mall. He stood most of the day while helping customers. After work, he would pick up the kids from school and they'd head home. Most nights, he'd eat dinner then rush to the garage to start his evening projects. He would mow grass for the elderly neighbors and fix broken items at our house or my parents' house next door, all while simultaneously keeping up with the maintenance of some rental property we owned close to our home. There was always much to do and he loved staying busy. So the night he came in from work and went straight to bed I thought perhaps, he was coming down with the flu.

The following day, it suddenly dawned on me that there could be something seriously wrong with Randy. We had ignored the signs for nearly six months. Randy had lost thirty pounds, his fatigue was getting worse, and his skin color had turned pale. He'd battled thyroid problems for years, which included multiple goiters located in his neck. He'd undergone biopsies on these goiters, which had all came back negative for cancer. This was always a concern for us, as several years earlier, Randy's father had been diagnosed with thyroid cancer and had his thyroid removed. After his surgery, Randy's dad had difficulty speaking without his voice cracking. Randy wanted no part of throat surgery until it was totally necessary, but we decided we could put it off no longer.

I scheduled an appointment for Randy with his endocrinologist, after which the doctor scheduled him for surgery to remove his thyroid in the coming weeks. One Friday night, a week before Randy's surgery, we went to the hospital for his surgery prep, which included a complete blood workup. All of his blood numbers were half the levels they should have been. This alarmed the hospital staff, which in turn alarmed us. They rushed Randy immediately to the emergency room for a blood transfusion. The ER staff wanted to admit him after his transfusion, but he convinced them to let him see his primary care physician on Monday for her opinion first. He already had an appointment scheduled with her and he trusted her diagnosis. The staff obliged Randy, but said he couldn't have his thyroid surgery until his illness had been diagnosed.

The following Monday, Randy met with his primary care physician. She said would try to schedule an office appointment for him with a hematologist that week; if she could not, she would admit him to the hospital and we would see the hematologist on call. Randy could see the concern and urgency in her eyes. He knew this could be a serious condition.

After a few days of waiting, our primary care doctor called to tell us she had been unable to locate a hematologist who had an open appointment to examine Randy. She'd scheduled him to be admitted to the hospital the following morning, where he would undergo a complete battery of tests so a diagnosis could be made of his symptoms.

When I look back at this time, I realize we still were oblivious to his situation. Neither of us became overly excited. We knew it couldn't be serious. He was too young and had been extremely healthy before. We were sure they were overreacting. He would check into the hospital, they would discover it was his thyroid wreaking havoc after all, and would then schedule him for thyroid surgery. How often does a serious illness strike a middle-age healthy person out of nowhere? Every now and then, we would hear a tragic story about someone else, but it wouldn't happen to us. Randy was too healthy. We truly had no clue.

After a few days in the hospital, many blood tests, x-rays, and even a bone marrow biopsy, no cancer could be found. We were thrilled. Exactly as we thought, it was an overreaction. The hematologist sent us home and told Randy he had the bone marrow of an anorexia teenager. The doctor felt Randy needed to eat healthier, perhaps more nutritious foods, and he would see us in two weeks to follow up on his progress. These were instructions we could easily follow to correct the situation. We believed every aspect of our lives would return to normal after a couple weeks of living a healthier lifestyle. Many times when you are new to the major illness scene, you observe through reluctant eyes. You see what you want to see. I thought Randy was too young and healthy to get cancer, even though I knew children and teenagers were diagnosed with this disease all the time. The thought never occurred to me that there could be a possibility his doctor was wrong. The diagnosis he made was the one we wanted to hear.

When we arrived home from the hospital, I began a mission of healthy eating for the entire family. I believed Randy had a fairly healthy diet already, but there were areas of possible improvements. He could have eaten more greens, which can be said for most of us, but I was more than ready to try the hematologist's solution. I made sure his diet consisted of lean meats, fresh fruits and vegetables, and whole grains for the next two weeks. No cheating was tolerated. He ate strictly healthy foods, a diet fit for an athlete, with no soft drinks or sugary foods. After two weeks, we returned to the doctor, who discovered after further bloodwork that Randy had experienced no improvement. The hematologist said it could take more time to see results. I looked at Randy as he talked to the doctor. He was just as tired, just as pale, and getting weaker. It was time to try a different direction. We decided to call Duke University Hospital.

Randy's mother had passed away several years earlier from Renal Cell Carcinoma, otherwise known as kidney cancer. She had traveled to Durham, North Carolina to go to Duke Hospital for cutting-edge treatment. Upon her diagnosis, she was given five years to live, but with the new treatments, who knows? She responded wonderfully. She eventually succumbed to her disease ten years later, but not without a fight. She tried all the latest treatments and trials Duke recommended. Our entire family had been extremely impressed with her care while she was at Duke battling this horrific disease.

Two weeks after we made the call to Duke, we drove to the hospital clinics in Durham, where we had appointments scheduled. We were first sent to the Hematology/Oncology department, due to Randy's current symptoms. The physician's assistant examined Randy and looked at the bloodwork Duke had done. She pressed around on his stomach area and could feel his spleen was enlarged. As she wrote something down on his paperwork, she appeared as though she knew the diagnosis. We asked if she could tell what was wrong, and she said we would discuss his case when the doctor came in. She clearly had an idea about the problem. I gave Randy a thumbs up. We were getting somewhere.

The doctor stepped into the room a short time later and reexamined Randy. He told us he felt sure Randy had *myelofibrosis*, which was a new word with no definition for us. He explained it was a pre-leukemia, which is why no cancer had showed in Randy's bone marrow biopsy. To put it in terms we could understand, he explained it was a scarring of the bone marrow. His marrow was so clogged with scar tissue, it couldn't produce new blood. The doctor would order further bloodwork to confirm his diagnosis, but the only course of treatment with a cure was a bone marrow or stem cell transplant. He would schedule the next available appointment at Duke's Adult Bone Marrow Transplant Clinic (ABMT), and said he would call us as soon as he received a confirmation from the bloodwork.

Then, the ABMT Clinic would take Randy's case through the next phase of his illness.

We thanked the doctor for seeing us and told him how pleased we were to have a diagnosis. We expressed our happiness that there was a possible cure. I asked the PA how to spell *myelofibrosis*. As she spelled the word for me, the doctor told us not to look it up on the internet. There was too much incorrect information to be found there. As soon as we drove the four and a half hours back to Charleston, I immediately looked it up on the internet.

Within the next few weeks, we were back at the ABMT Clinic for our initial appointment. They had the results of Randy's extensive bloodwork and found that he did indeed have myelofibrosis and would need a bone marrow/stem cell transplant. We had many meetings with doctors, physician assistants, social workers, and finance/insurance advisors. It was explained to us, Randy would be in the hospital approximately four weeks. He would then need to remain in the Durham, North Carolina area for another three to four months so he could be in clinic every day to monitor his progress.

Over the three to four months of clinic visits, the daily visits would become every other day, then every three days, et cetera, depending on his improvement. The doctor explained to us that this treatment schedule would be in place if Randy's response to the treatment went according to plan. We did not discuss the alternative. Randy and I decided we would leave his illness, the expenses, and our much-needed help in the Lord's hands. We would remain positive and battle this illness together with every ounce of our strength. We believed we were in good hands with an experienced team at Duke.

We drove home after the ABMT clinic appointment, discussing our options. We were encouraged by the doctor's belief that the transplant would remedy his illness. Randy's only sibling, his brother Doug, told us he would be happy to donate bone marrow if he was a match for Randy's markers. Doug said, "I'll give you my right arm if you need it." We knew he meant it.

Duke told us to bring Doug to the next appointment so they could check his blood to see if he was a match. In bone marrow donation, the possibility of an acceptable match by a sibling is one in four. Unfortunately, Doug was not a match. We had hit a setback right out of the gate, but we still could check for a match in the blood marrow bank. There were six million samples in storage at that time. Duke would compare Randy's bloodwork with the samples in the bank the following week to look for a perfect match. They would call us when and if they found one.

The phone rang the following week. Randy had two perfect matches and one was willing to donate. We found out a year later, the donor was a former Marine and current fireman who lived in California. Thank you, Lord and thank you, Steve.

Duke explained to us that Randy was young at forty-eight years old, in good health besides this disease, and had the right attitude. The doctors told us he had an 80 percent chance of survival, but it would be a tough road. He would get high-dose chemotherapy while he was in the hospital, which would take his white blood cell count to zero. The hospital would continually monitor him for infection, and after the transplant they would also watch for graft-versus-host-disease. Again, another medical term we had never before encountered.

Graft-versus-host-disease (GvHD) is a complication that can occur after the bone marrow/stem cell transplant in which the new transplanted cells see the recipient's body as foreign to them. When this happens, the newly transplanted cells attack the recipient's body. GvHD can show itself in a mild form, such as a skin rash, to a severe case, which can damage body organs, or anywhere in between.

I listened to the professionals explain the many medical terms of this condition. Most of these terms, I was unfamiliar with, so I decided we would worry about GvHD if and when it happened. I immediately dismissed them in my mind. We would worry about complications as they occurred. I decided I was not going to drive myself crazy over *what if*. There were too many "what ifs" with this disease. It was too much to process, and I encourage you to not let the enormity of your own situation overwhelm you. Prioritize what is important to you now, and leave the rest for the Lord to sort out. Trust that He will only allow what you can handle.

Duke gave us a notebook to answer many of our questions about the treatment. It was 111 pages long. I read it three times and was thankful for every page. Randy never opened the notebook and didn't want me to tell him any more than generalities about the procedure. The notebook was invaluable to me. It described his disease, the stem cells, and gave reasons why a transplant was needed. It explained how they identify a donor and how both the patient and the donor are evaluated.

The most important part was toward the end of the notebook, which explained the patient's role in a successful transplant and how to prepare for it. Reading this notebook was a must for the patient, but Randy didn't want to read it. The thought of what those pages contained made Randy extremely uncomfortable. He didn't want to know about any painful procedures that could possibly come his way. He had spoken earlier to another caregiver of a bone marrow transplant patient. He asked her to describe what the patient went through. "Hell," she replied. That patient ended up dying. I know this was why Randy didn't want to know the details.

Before he began his transplant, Randy came to his senses and realized maybe he should know a little about the process. He asked me about the hospital stay, which occurred at the beginning of the transplant. His question opened the door for me to tell him bits and pieces of the positive details, of which he had to look forward. Perhaps *look forward to* is an overreach, but I wanted him to look at the transplant as a positive solution because there was a really good chance it would cure him.

In my mind, every bit of information contained in that notebook was positive because it was a roadmap to a successful transplant. It did contain information on "Being a Survivor," which described possible suppressed emotions, which could surface later. These could include anger, anxiety, or depression, as well as guilt and grief. I'm the type who wants to know all possible outcomes so I can watch for a negative downturn and call the doctor, whether it's physical or if it's emotional. I would now know after reading the notebook what to expect. I understand we are all not wired this way—Randy is not.

When you are the caregiver and not the patient, it is important to be sensitive to the differences between you and the patient. At this stage of the illness, it was about what was best for him, physically and emotionally, not what was best for me. Randy wanted to remain completely positive, so I satisfied my desire to know every detail by reading the notebook to myself, but I only told him specific information when he asked. This was the way he wanted it. He would ask questions as he was ready. But I knew when he asked the questions, he was looking for reassurance, not concerns.

I had many questions that were not answered in the notebook. I couldn't even locate possible answers to my questions on the "forbidden" internet. I know this because after I searched online, I found out every patient really is different; the doctors were not just telling us this. Even still, it was not for a lack of trying. I wanted to know the side effects of the high-dose chemo, what happens immediately before the patient receives the marrow transplant, what does marrow look like, and does it change your DNA or blood type. There were too many questions. I searched fervently, but I could not find one patient with the same symptoms as Randy. His illness was unique. When we saw the doctor or PA, if I had questions with a possible negative answer, I never asked them in front of Randy. Nothing I wanted to know was worth upsetting him. If it was a question that had no bearing on his outcome, I never asked it. Too many questions were wearisome for Randy. Duke made sure we knew all the imperative answers; everything else, I kept to myself or did my own research.

A devastating illness can take a toll on everyone in the family. Randy's disease required both of us to be gone for an extended period of time. There would be medical bills, rent, food, and travel expenses. His illness was taking both of us out of the workforce for the time we'd be away. We were going to need some help. The following are some helpful suggestions that other kind individuals recommended as well as some I developed on my own. I hope they help you as much as they did me.

YOU CAN'T DO IT ALONE

L isten to me. This is the most important thing I will tell you. *You have to get some help.* If you plan on trying to tackle your loved one's illness without assistance, you most likely will burn out. For example, you might take a walk one day and forget to return home. This may sound dramatic, but you will find yourself extremely overwhelmed, which will result in your inability to be the kind of caregiver your loved one needs. You want to be at your best when they are at their weakest. If they see you marching toward the battle, it will give them strength to do the same. What if you have no one? Find someone, even if you have to hire them for a couple hours each day. I know this is easier said than done, but there are kind people who are always willing to lend (or loan) a hand. We are thankful for our support team, which included our faith, our family, and our friends.

First and foremost, our faith supported us throughout this long and trying ordeal. The greatest aspect of having faith in your life is you are never alone. God is always with you. He is there for the worst days and the best days. Days when you don't think you can make it another moment, He gives you the strength to carry on. Days when you see progress in your loved one's recovery, God is there to rejoice with you. While Randy was in the hospital, he had days of complications and setbacks, as well as many days with positive and encouraging results. God and I had many conversations. Talking to my Lord and letting him know what I was feeling, calmed me. Telling Him my concerns, worries and fears got me through the dark and murky days. While at Duke I did a lot of reading in Psalms about the promises God has made to us. I knew no matter what the prognosis, God would be with us. Trust in the Lord and don't get so bogged down that you forget your alone time with Him. Faith is first on my help list for a reason. It's the support we can't do without.

Secondly, more often than not, your family is there for you. While every family member may not be able to be physically present, in most cases, you can find a special someone who will be there when you need them most. It may even be a surprising someone. Perhaps a member of the family who you would never have dreamed would step up. In our case, at the beginning, it was not a surprise; it was my mother. While we were at Duke, my mother traded places with me every other week for the four weeks Randy was in the hospital. It was imperative that I periodically return home for our three teenagers, Sam, Alex and Rachel, as well as my responsibilities of running a weekly payroll at work. It was impossible for me to stay away for four weeks. After Randy's hospital stay, we were still looking at three to four months of clinic visits nearly every day in Durham, North Carolina. My mom and I had to find more help. After we made our help request known to the family, Randy's Uncle Phil called and said he would be there for us and to just say when.

Randy and his Uncle Phil had a typical uncle/nephew relationship before the illness. We saw him on holidays and at funerals and weddings. Phil was a retired truck driver and teamster with two children who were grown. He and his wife, Christene, lived about thirty minutes away from our house, about half the distance between Charleston and Huntington. Phil and Randy were both jokesters, so I felt like Phil's presence would be a welcomed change for Randy in the rotation of me and my mother. Little did I know how close they would become. Uncle Phil stepped into the parental void that was left when Randy's mother had passed away five years earlier, as Randy's relationship with his father was nonexistent. Uncle Phil was Randy's mother's brother which gave him that connection to his much-loved mother who was no longer with us.

On most days, Phil kept Randy walking and exploring the Durham tourist spots whenever he was physically able. Phil always kept himself physically fit and he expected Randy to do the same. This supplemental physical activity was extremely beneficial to Randy's overall health. Even more importantly, Phil would crack jokes most of the day and kept Randy's mind off his wearisome ordeal. Randy would call me from Duke and describe to me how he and Uncle Phil were nearly kicked out of clinic due to cutting up too much. He was just kidding of course, but they enjoyed stirring things up. Duke loved to see their patients having a good time because it's contagious.

Uncle Phil was there for us during the clinic rotations and also later on when Randy had complications. He never let Randy wallow in self-pity and he kept him physically working out. I don't know how we would have made it without him. We cannot forget the sacrifice of his wife, Christene, who was willing to be home alone all those times Phil was out of town with Randy. God had provided a truly special couple to walk through this trying time with us.

We received many phone calls and well-wishing cards from family and friends who could not be with Randy at Duke, but wanted to let him know they were thinking of him and praying for his recovery. This was a significant part of Randy's caregiving as well. Randy's aunts and cousins on his mother's side checked in with him regularly, as well as our siblings on both sides. My family continually called as well.

This always lifted Randy's spirits, as well as my own, knowing we were cared and prayed for.

As you walk through your own journey, encourage your family to check in regularly with your loved one. Make sure the patient has their own cell phone so they can be reached at most times of their day. When they do not feel like talking, turn the phone off to only receive voicemails and text messages. The patient can return the calls and texts at their convenience. Whenever possible, let the patient handle their own phone conversations and texts. I have seen instances in which the caregiver would screen the calls of the sick. This takes away the patient's independence and makes them feel even less in charge of their daily activities. Let the patient decide when they want to accept or return calls and messages.

Allowing the patient to retain some control over their life gives them a feeling of empowerment at a time when so many situations are out of their control. This will also take a great deal of responsibility off you, as the caregiver, to keep everyone updated on the patient's progress. Let your loved one make the calls. Then they feel as though others are interested in their wellbeing and allows them to feel useful. They will have phone calls to return on most days when they feel up to it.

Symptoms change quite often during a major illness. Friends and relatives like to stay current on the improvements and setbacks. Your loved one will have more calls to return than time to make them. My husband loves talking on the phone, so this strategy worked well for us. If your loved one is not a phone person, they can send emails or text messages. Tweak this suggestion to fit your situation. Having the patient reply to concerned friends and family will also allow you some extra time for yourself to recoup your rest and energy.

Lastly, but not the least example, some cherished friends were always there for us from the beginning of Randy's illness, and they remain with us today. It was a dear friend from church also named Philip (not to confuse with Uncle Phil) who was a spiritual anchor for Randy even before he was diagnosed with his illness. He was an older gentleman who had worked with my dad for over thirty years at the telephone company. He went to church with my parents and had also known Randy's parents. After Randy was diagnosed, Philip would bring Randy milkshakes and sit with him in the infusion center of the hospital while he received blood transfusions. He called him nearly every day during his illness at Duke and continues to call him today. If Randy doesn't hear from him by early evening, he will call and check on Philip, who has had some health issues himself. I'm amazed at the difference one caring individual can make in the life of another.

Another couple, Jack and Cheryl, made inquiring calls to help us select the correct doctors at Duke; they made a special trip to Durham to see Randy while he was in clinic and helped us on the home front with yard work and maintaining our rental property. Our friends Bud and Patty made the trip to North Carolina to visit Randy and pray with him. We enjoyed seeing both couples immensely. In addition, the outpouring of get well cards and phone calls from many other friends from work and church meant the world to Randy. He looked forward to opening them daily and reminiscing about the senders.

When I wasn't at Duke with Randy, I tried to take care of the maintenance at home with the help of the kids. Our sons were both in college by the time Randy had his GVHD relapse and was back at Duke recovering with Uncle Phil standing watch. Having no sons around created difficulties in trying to accomplish the tasks Randy normally handled. Before the illness, I never gave these jobs a second thought because Randy made sure they were always done. Our youngest daughter, Rachel and I decided this would be no big deal; we could handle the yard work.

I've always had this over-inflated confidence that if I start a project, problems will resolve themselves and eventually the task will be complete. You just have to get started. My way of thinking is to remain diligent and keep working. I know I'm this way because Randy has always been there to fix what I start but can't finish so things always do work themselves out—only it's Randy doing the fixing, rather than the problems miraculously working themselves out. Even though Randy wasn't around at this time, I knew things would be fine, but in reality, things were never fine.

We had problems every time we tried to take care of anything. It seems no matter what man-chore we attempted during these women-only times, someone always showed up to help at just the moment we were about to make a complete mess of the situation. I know some ladies can manage these chores without a fella and I don't want to offend them, but I didn't have the training. Rachel and I were both rookies in the yard and car departments, but we were learning.

I remember several times having trouble starting the lawn mower when Randy was at Duke for a second extended stay and my sons were away. Rachel and I would be out in the driveway, pulling on the starter until we were blue in the face. Without fail, someone would always be passing by the house who would happily lend us a hand. Rachel and I would take turns pushing the lawn mower. We were a pitiful sight. It would take us a couple days but eventually we would finish the job. A sweet couple, Charles and Verna, lived in one of our rental townhouses. Each week, they came over to the house to get our lawnmower and mow the grass around the townhouses. They were so caring and thoughtful during Randy's illness. It would have been extremely difficult without their kindness.

My last suggestion must include my husband's love of receiving candy during his hospital and clinic stay. His day was made anytime someone brought him a box of chocolates or a candy bar. He would save them for later in the day as a dessert. I noticed how he looked forward to his sweet treat, so I would try to bring him something sweet and different each day.

One day, Randy's only brother, Doug and his wife, Jill visited him at Duke and brought him a large bag of candy. It looked like a bag the kids would bring home on Halloween. This bag included an assortment of gums, rolls of hard candy, mints, and various candy bars. It was his favorite gift during his entire stay at Duke.

For many chronically ill patients, candy may brighten their day but be sure to first check if their medical diet allows it. Most of us are still children at heart and we never forget how candy brought us smiles when we were younger. It probably goes without saying; candy goes a long way with the caregiver too. (Hint) On many occasions I could be found digging through that candy bag when no one was looking. Randy caught Uncle Phil in the candy bag more than once as well. I don't believe any of us, no matter how old we get, ever grow out of our love of candy.

Perhaps candy isn't your loved one's craving. Find out what gesture makes that person happy and be sure they get plenty of it. Even small pleasures make a difference when fighting a severe illness.

When you are caring for a loved one, gladly accept help from friends and family. Most severe illnesses are long term, so your resources can run thin over time. If anyone asks, encourage cards, as well as well-wishing phone calls (and candy or anything else that brings the patient joy). When your patient finds delight in small gestures, it produces big results.

FIND JOY EVERY DAY

Being a daily caregiver, no matter how vital your role, can become monotonous and mundane. When Randy was in the hospital for his first four-week stay, my days were busy and productive. Every other day I washed his laundry at a public laundromat in my hotel. I constantly ran after food for him when he didn't feel like eating what the hospital provided. I wanted him to keep his strength up, so I'd go find whatever he found appetizing that day. I kept him on schedule with his daily walking exercises in the hospital halls and his personal grooming. There was always something to do to keep us busy.

After Randy's first four weeks in the Duke Hospital, we immediately started his clinic visits. We moved from the hotel (me) and hospital (him) to a short-stay, furnished apartment. Thankfully it included a washer and dryer, so I no longer needed to go out to do our laundry. We regularly cooked in the apartment so we could be sure all Randy's sanitary restrictions were met during food prep. Randy was often too weak to go out, but he could take short trips to the grocery store with me and go on his exercise walk each evening. His only requirement was he had to wear his face mask whenever he was out.

During our stay at the apartment, the repetition of my daily activities began to wear on me. After breakfast, I would spend thirty minutes straightening up the apartment and doing whatever small tasks needed to be accomplished that day. If it wasn't a grocery store or doctor visit day, it could prove to be a very long twenty-four hours. I realized very quickly that I would need to find some joy for my days.

You may find funny what proved to be joy for me. It was small things spread throughout my day to which I could look forward. I drink coffee every morning, which I thoroughly enjoy. I added a cup after dinner while I read my emails or the local newspaper. I looked forward to this. I realized another joy for me was at Duke Hospital. They had a yogurt/fresh fruit/granola cup in their first-floor cafeteria that I would eat for lunch most days while Randy was in the hospital. There were times I didn't feel like eating a heavy lunch and the yogurt cup was filling without being too much. I found

I missed this small treat. So, I added it to my weekly joy regimen. On days when Randy had clinic, I would swing by the hospital and grab a yogurt with fresh blueberries and granola. Randy couldn't believe I would go to the extra trouble to run in the cafeteria and pick up their yogurt when I could buy yogurt at the store. But store bought wasn't as good. This yogurt brought me joy.

I know what you're thinking. *Does all her joy involve food or drink?* No, but nutrition is a worthy starting point for joy because we all have our favorites. We don't have to contemplate long to think of something delicious that makes us happy. Look for something that won't create another problem, such as weight gain or high cholesterol. If a high -calorie item brings you joy, eat it once a week or in small quantities.

Another joy for me is learning new things. I did a search on the internet while we were in Durham and found a local museum and some local tourist sites that looked interesting. We found a museum with history about the Durham area and information about local animals.

Another fun excursion for us involved Randy's restrictions with his diet. He had some strict food guidelines so we would frequent a Whole Foods or Trader Joe's in the area and search for some new and healthy items he could try. We do not have a Whole Foods or Trader Joe's in Charleston, so this was a fun, new experience for us.

More than once during these short trips to the stores and the museums, Randy would need to go back to the car to sit and rest. You will need to work around the specific wellness guidelines of your loved ones illness. Try to go together on your get-out-of-the-house trips. Work in both your interests, but also be aware there will be times your loved one cannot go or will require a slower pace.

There were days when Randy was too weak, or his blood count numbers weren't what they should be. I could tell if it was necessary for me to stay in the apartment with him, or if he was well enough for me to step out for a much-needed breather. Use your judgement. It's a balancing act that you as the caregiver will need to do. You don't want to leave your loved one if it's risky for them to be alone, but there will be times you can get away by yourself for a couple hours. If they need constant care, make sure you schedule a relief person who will allow a break throughout the day for yourself, or at least one day off during the week. If you are at your best, it will show in the care you give.

When Randy's Uncle Phil came down for a rotation, he would take Randy exploring. They would jump in Phil's truck and take off driving. Sometimes they would visit historical sites, other times they would drive just to see what they could find along the way. Several times this resulted in them becoming lost and needing to stop and ask directions. Eventually, Uncle Phil bought a GPS, which helped during their adventures. They had many escapades during their trips around town. By the end of Randy's Duke Clinic stay, he and Phil could traverse the Durham roads as if they lived there. Uncle Phil had the uncanny ability to find his joy through adventures. What he had no way of knowing, in finding his joy, he found Randy's joy also.

I cannot end this chapter about joy without mentioning my favorite pastime, reading. Books are another area in which I find my joy. I'm always frequenting library sales or buying books that interest me when I can get a good buy. I have many books in my home that I have not had time to read but would love to one day. I took about ten with me for the apartment stay in Durham. On days when Randy felt better, we would go to the closest bookstore and look around for an hour or two. Randy would plant himself in a chair beside the magazines racks with his mask on and ignore the stares. I would scurry down the aisles, looking for sale stickers. History and biographies are my passion so I would always head to those departments. Many times I would come to the counter with another book I would hope to someday find the time to read. (Joy!)

If I woke up before Randy, I would try to take advantage of my alone time to read my Bible. Psalms was my book of choice during Randy's long illness, due to the promises enclosed within its pages. I love Psalm 23 because it takes us away from present circumstances to a calm, green meadow where Christ is our Shepherd and we shall not want. Include your faith when you're selecting what brings you joy. A daily Bible devotion will sustain you and take you farther than any cup of coffee or yogurt parfait ever will.

Find some special items, excursions, or devotions that will bring you joy every day. Better yet, come up with something completely out of your comfort zone that you have always wanted to try and do it! Find something new that will bring you joy. Like I said earlier, it doesn't have to be something large and life changing, just as long as it lifts your spirit and gives you added strength to take on the day.

FULL-TIME JOB,
PART-TIME CAREGIVER

Are you someone who works all day at your job, then comes home as a part-time caregiver of your spouse, parent, child, or sibling? My heart goes out to you. I understand this difficult situation. Not only do you work 9-5 at your day job, afterward you come to more work waiting on your arrival. And this work you cannot put off until the next day.

When we arrived back in Charleston after Randy's four-month hospital and clinic stay following his transplant, we thought he would be on the quick road to recovery. Why wouldn't he be? We did everything the doctor told us. Randy took his medicines on time and followed all the post-transplant instructions as far as avoiding crowds and exercising regularly whenever possible. *Wrong*.

Randy developed Graft-versus-host-disease, a common complication to an allogenic bone marrow transplant and the same disease the doctor had previously told us could occur during or after Randy's treatment. GvHD can show itself in many forms, such as a mild rash to severe gastro problems, and even organ damage. Randy developed the severe gastro form. His symptoms amounted to an extremely irritable bowel, which resulted in him running to the bathroom every time he ate. He would lose his food immediately after he had eaten.

This went on for a couple days and he was getting worse. At the time, we didn't know it was GvHD. I thought he caught a stomach bug. When he started getting dehydrated and loopy, I knew we had to act immediately. I called Duke and told them something was seriously wrong. His symptoms were lasting too long; it couldn't be just a virus. They had us return to Durham immediately, which resulted in another hospital stay and more clinic time. Randy was so sick, he could not have survived without returning to the Duke clinic. Uncle Phil came to the rescue again and rotated with me so I could come home every other week.

When Randy came home after the GvHD setback, he was in terrible shape. He had been on high-dose steroids to counter the effects of the disease and had lost another fifty pounds, in addition to the fifty pounds he had lost before and during the transplant. He was weak and in constant pain. His doctors gave him pain medicine and still ran tests to determine the extent of the damage to his intestines.

During this trying time, Randy took a morphine pill when the pain was more than he could bear. We also noticed he began throwing up immediately after he ate. We didn't put the two events together. There were so many new variables in the mix now that it wasn't obvious. He continued to lose weight. It took us several weeks to figure it out; the morphine was causing him to throw up. He didn't throw up immediately after taking the pill; it could be four or five hours later when he ate. We thought perhaps it was something he was eating that wasn't agreeing with him. Wrong again. He stopped taking the morphine and the throwing up ceased. My mother figured this out for us. She told me she had never been able to take morphine for pain because it made her stomach upset. She was right. Never underestimate the advice of your elders. Listen when they speak to you. They have been on this earth longer and most have more wisdom and intelligence to show for it.

Randy would have to take something else for the pain. His sensitive stomach kept him from being able to take much of anything for his discomfort. I wondered if he would ever get better. He was 6'1" and weighed 150 pounds. He looked like a holocaust survivor. He had lost 110 pounds since the beginning of the transplant. It was heartbreaking.

This was an incredibly stressful time for me. It killed me to see Randy in so much pain and I felt as though there was nothing I could do. None of the medicines relieved his suffering unless it put him to sleep. I would come home from work and try to make him comfortable. I tried to buy foods I knew he liked, then I would tell him uplifting or funny stories from work. He would try to smile. There were days when I would run to the pharmacy on the way home to pick up some new prescriptions the doctors adjusted to his changing symptoms. We would go over how often he needed to take his new medicine and put it in his pill dispenser for the next two weeks. I would help the kids with their homework, take a shower, and fall into the bed so I could sleep, then wake up and do it all over again.

My greatest recommendation for you during this time is to, again, find some help. Share the workload with whoever will help. Since it was my husband who was sick, I enlisted our teenage children, my parents and my sister, Randy's brother, and always Uncle Phil. They helped me with cooking, yard work, errands, and doctor appointments. If you are working and caregiving, you absolutely cannot do it alone. The illness alone is difficult enough, so when you have help, take the assistance. It will help you get through your day and give your God-given helpers a feeling of gratification for supporting the two of you.

Remember, people cannot read your mind. If you don't tell your family and friends you need help, they will never know. Some may offer, but others may think you don't want to be bothered with more people in your home. You have to speak up and let them know where you need the most help.

Next, you will need to remove yourself from the sickness for a few minutes each day and find some time on your own not related to work or sickness. We have two dogs—a have a golden retriever named Daisy who was eight at the time and weighed ninety pounds, and a cavachon named Penny who was five and a chunky twenty-two pounds—that needed to go on a walk each evening. The kids always volunteered to take this chore off my plate, but little did they know I needed to go on a walk as much as the dogs.

Daisy, the golden, knows what I want her to do before I even say it. When I grab her leash, she comes over for me to hook her up and start the walk. As we walk, she stays to the right side and in the grass away from the cars. Then there's Penny. She never comes over for me to hook up her harness. I always have to go get her. While we're walking, she turns around every five seconds to see if anyone is walking behind us so she can bark like a crazed animal that has lost her mind.

I constantly pull on Penny's harness to get her to turn around (which she will never do until the other walkers stroll pass us). Then barks ferociously the entire time they walk around us. Afterward, an overly-satisfied look crosses her face, as if she has saved our lives. In her mind, she knew the other walkers were up to no good. This usually prompts Daisy to nip at Penny to stop acting like a fool. Daisy acts as if Penny's behavior embarrasses her and she's not putting up with it any longer. The golden looks up at me as if to say, "Can you do something?" I can't. As soon as the other walkers pass us and are ahead about twenty feet, Penny immediately begins turning around every five seconds again, looking for someone else to bark at.

This is the daily comical distraction I needed. It might not sound entertaining to you, but I never knew what bazaar behavior Penny would demonstrate each day. I only knew it would not involve her following the rules and being obedient. This stroll with the dogs took me away from the caregiving at home and put me into less serious, more humorous mindset for a few minutes, which I always enjoyed.

During Randy's recovery, I usually walked the dogs with one of my teenagers and we would discuss their day. I could always get more out of them when we were one-on-one. Rarely would they want to bother us with their problems while Randy was sick because we had so much to deal with daily. But when it was just me and one of them, they would tell me about their day, good and bad. I cherished those walks. Sometimes we would see other walkers who would stop and say hello and ask about Randy. I was usually out of the house about forty-five minutes to an hour, not long at all. And I would go after Randy had eaten supper and was resting.

If you are caregiving in your own home, find your needed distraction, even for just a few minutes each day to take some time for yourself. If not a pet, as in our situation, whatever you can focus on apart from caregiving is what I suggest. In our case, it was our dogs. I'm not saying get a dog because they are a lot of extra work, but the dogs worked splendidly in my situation. We had plenty of family members to help with the animals when we were out of town and the interaction between people and animals can be so comforting and calming. A pet in your home also means your loved one is never alone.

Proceed cautiously if you are looking for an animal buddy. I have seen pets come into a home where there was no illness and completely destroy the house and the relationships within it. I have also seen the positive side, with the animal becoming a wonderful companion. They keep the patient preoccupied with their antics and they demand attention from your loved one. The pet doesn't see the patient as ill. They are simply another human who can play and get them treats. When Randy was able, he would help us with the animals by letting them outside or filling their water bowl. He would fuss at them and tell them how much trouble they were. Then, they would give him a big lick on the foot and all was forgotten. A calm and loving pet can be there to distract and comfort your loved one, so they are not constantly dwelling on their illness. There are substantial benefits for caregiver and patient alike.

POCAHONTAS

When our kids were little, establishing a family code word was a popular thing to do. It was a word or phrase of which only the family was aware. When the word was used, it always meant the message was authentic. Our word was *Pocahontas*. We believed it was an ideal code word because it wasn't common and the kids were able to work it into phrases if necessary. Our children loved the movie, which was a plus, and each child had seen it multiple times. The film even has a historical reference from our nation's past so it was educational. What more could you want from a code word?

We gave our children the same warnings as every other parent with children born in the 1990s. *Don't go anywhere with strangers; don't help anyone find their lost puppy; and don't tell anyone our code word. If we send someone different to pick you up from school, or we send word for you to go home with another student, whoever gives you this message will know the code word.* You have to remember, this was a time before every child's backpack contained a cell phone.

Needless to say, we never had to use the code word with the kids so it became an object of laughter among our family. The word turned into a comical but serious plea for help when the kids were teenagers. The word would come up if one of us found ourselves in a jam and needed help to get out. These weren't tough jams, mostly getting caught in detention hall or stuck with someone they did not want to be with. The rest of us would see a sudden *Pocahontas* appear in a text or during a phone call.

On other occasions, one of the kids would call home on their lunch break from school on a particularly tough day and claim, "Pocahontas!" We would reply, "Why? What's wrong?" The underlying meaning was, "If there is any way possible, could someone rescue me." If we heard *Pocahontas*, we knew it wasn't being used lightly. They weren't joking around. We didn't get too many, but every now and then, the kids would use the word to reinforce the seriousness of whatever the situation.

Even today, Randy and I still use the word, and especially when he was sick. During his first four-week stint in the hospital, if he was having painful treatments before I arrived in the morning, he might text me, "Pocahontas!" I didn't know what was happening to him at the time; I only knew he needed me to be there quickly.

This chapter may work for some of you and for others it will not. My immediate family is a light-hearted bunch and we don't get mad easily. We liked the fact that we had a word that, if used by one of us, the others would come running. But there are situations when code words are not needed and inappropriate. When Randy went through his GvHD setback, conditions were dire. We weren't joking around much. During this time, Randy had no problems conveying exactly what he wanted done without a code word. He didn't have the extra energy.

If your loved one is at a place when establishing a code word between you will work, pick one out together. Establish what using the word will imply and have fun. Make the code word something that has meaning to the two of you. If a close friend or family member discovers your word, you may want to let them in on the secret. Our niece, Jordan, discovered our code word one day when she was in on a discussion we were having about an occasion when we used the word. Now she has adopted the word too. When she's in a tense situation and she wants to tell us about it, she will text us, "Pocahontas." It's amazing how one random word can take on special meaning for a family and bring everyone closer together.

MACKINAC ISLAND

I am the queen of redirection. This is a skill I acquired while our three children were little and all wanted to play with the same toy at exactly the same time. When everyone wanted to peddle the same toy car or fight with the same toy sword, Mom would quickly find an alternative to make one of them happy. I would grab a basketball and start dribbling it in a circle as if it were the best toy ever invented. My oldest son, Sam, would look at me like I was crazy, but I could usually get one of the younger two to join in.

I would also use this skill to calm the kids if they ever felt uncomfortable in what they deemed a scary situation. When the children were nine, seven, and four, we took them to St. Louis for a booksellers' trade show. We always took our family with us whenever we went out of town for business or pleasure, and I credit this to one of the reasons why we are so close today. Now, we still laugh often about past trips when we were all together and ended up in some crazy mess. It usually resulted from having children who were too young to be on a business trip, but that's just the way we roll.

During the St. Louis trip, Randy and I would spend the morning at the show (kids in tow), and the afternoon running around sightseeing. We knew we didn't want to leave town without visiting the St. Louis Arch. Inside the tour building was truly impressive. Randy and I watched the short movie about the history and building of the arch, but the kids were less interested. They sat still for a few minutes, then slowly began fidgeting. The longer the movie went, the more they moved. It was obvious we were disrupting those around us. We decided to skip the rest and go ahead and take them up in the arch.

I assumed there was an elevator, but I hadn't thought it through. The staff put us in these small, circular lifts that only held two people. Randy and our oldest son, Sam, got in one and I rode up with our middle son, Alex, and daughter, Rachel. It was a tight fit for all of us and it even made me somewhat claustrophobic. I hoped it would rise quickly. It didn't. We started moving up while a constant clicking noise *click click clicked*, as if we were on a roller coaster climbing toward a drop. I noticed the kids' worried looks. They needed to think about something else.

When I was young, before I had started school, my dad taught me to spell *Mississippi*. He'd have me spell it for every adult we encountered. I would happily stand and rattle off the spelling of Mississippi, impressed with my four-year-old self while basking in their praise of what a smart little girl I was.

While we rode up the arch, I noticed we could see the Mississippi River out the little window on the door. I decided to use my dad's tactics and teach my kids to spell Mississippi. We made it fun, like a rhyme, and gave it some rhythm. Those kids were spelling Mississippi like pros when we got off the lift at the top. They ran to their dad and spelled it for him. Randy shot me a confused look. The kids were proud of themselves and the worry had disappeared. Redirection is a must if you are a parent.

Another instance of redirection involves Mackinac Island, which is a place our family loves to visit. It's a small island in Lake Huron at the top of Michigan, just below the Upper Peninsula. We try to go every year and it's always something the kids look forward to. There are no cars allowed on the island, except for an ambulance, fire truck, and a police car. The streets are full of horses and everyone rides bikes or walks wherever they need to go. The island is only eight miles around so no destination is too far.

Randy had been home for several months from his second stay at Duke during his relapse with GvHD, but he was still a long way from recovery. He was tired, I was tired, and the kids were tired. We all needed a change of atmosphere, change of venue, and most of all a change of attitude. I decided it was time for some redirection. It was summertime. We would pack the car and head to Mackinac Island for a week. The lake air would do us all good and lift our spirits.

Randy usually did most of the driving on our trips, but that was not going to be an option for us this time. Since he had been at Duke and we live in West Virginia, I had driven the four-and-a-half-hour trip to Durham, North Carolina many times by myself. I talked to the boys and they agreed to help me drive the ten-and-a-half-hour journey to Mackinac Island. Sam was in college now and Alex was ready to start. We loaded all the bikes, clothes, and snacks, and hit the road.

We left early in the morning, around five. We have a large express van, so there is plenty of room for the five of us plus the bikes. Sam sat up front with me and kept me company while everyone else slept. After grabbing breakfast at a drive-thru, and some seat changes (Rachel moved up front) we turned on some music from the kids' phones and took turns playing songs. When we grew tired of listening to music and the kids started getting restless, I told Rachel, who would soon begin eleventh grade, to grab one of the books I had brought along to read on the trip. I'm always buying books when our local library has their book sale once a year. If I see an author I am familiar with, I buy the book. They are extremely inexpensive and they sell them by the box. I always purchase several boxes each year.

One of these books was a mystery genre by an author I enjoyed reading. The only thing different about this book was he coauthored it with another person with whom I was not familiar. I was sure it was just as entertaining as his other books and would convey the same quality of work. This author's books always started with an exciting first chapter. I thought the kids could take turns reading, and all of us would enjoy something different. We would create our own audio book with our voices. I told Rachel to start reading the book out loud and we would all listen. Of course, the boys thought this was a dumbest idea they had ever heard and informed me they would not be taking part. I told them to try it, they might enjoy it. They groaned and laid back down in their seats.

The book started with a murder, which is the main author's *modus operandi*. After a couple more pages, I noticed Rachel slowing her reading to a pause. I asked her what was up. She said "Mom, some words in this book are not too nice." This shocked me. All of this author's books I had read earlier were fine. The murder was a bit graphic, but not over the top. I told her to skip over the curse words if there were any and if she read something that was not appropriate, substitute words that were. I was trying to come up with a way to salvage this idea and still have her read the book. I was sure the book wasn't that bad. Rachel agreed to give it a go.

She read a couple more sentences and I noticed the storyline was heading in a sexual direction. Rachel continued reading, "He noticed her tight sweater and her..." Rachel paused again, "…buttons were firm." I immediately saw both my boys' heads pop up from the back of the van. I knew she had substituted a word. I said, "That's enough reading for today." Randy popped his head out from under the covers and started laughing hysterically. He then proceeded to ask me what kind of books I was reading. Obviously, the coauthor had changed the writing style. We would need to choose another book. We were definitely distracted from the ever-looming illness. This comical situation was exactly what was needed after our ordeal, although it wasn't the type of distraction I would've planned.

When we arrived at Mackinac Island, there were adjustments which had to be made due to Randy's illness. He could not stand, sit, or walk for long periods of time, so we had to make sure anytime we were outside, there was a shaded place where he could rest. Since his transplant, he can never be in the sun for a prolonged amount of time. It can trigger GvHD. We did not want that setback to return. Randy could only ride his bike with us for a limited amount of time. I made sure he did not over exert himself and got plenty of rest. It was a much-needed change of scenery.

Don't be afraid to change the location for your loved one. They get tired of sitting in the same chair, day after day, just like you get tired of the same location, day after day. Take your loved one for a drive. Look at the changing leaves or just enjoy the beautiful, warm sunshine. Eat at a new restaurant. If your loved one is not able to go inside, get take out, but take them with you to pick up the food if possible. Get them out of the house.

Mix up their daily routine, as well as your own. If they normally watch baseball on television, turn on a soccer game or another new sport. Both of you can learn the rules of the game and enjoy something different. Buy a new board game. Many homebound and long-term illness patients enjoy board games and competition. I enjoy them, especially Parcheesi and Scrabble. They are stimulating and challenging. It creates a scenario in which your loved one can feel like a winner after they have many days of battling their illness and feeling as though they are not gaining ground (maybe every once in a while, you can win a game too). Create some distractions. It will be good for your loved one as well as yourself.

Perhaps your loved one would like a new puzzle. If not too frustrating, puzzles can be great fun. Every day, the patient will see the progress they have made and it will keep them from just sitting in front of the brain-numbing television. My family especially likes the White Mountain puzzles with the larger pieces, even the teenagers. We try to buy a new one every few months. It will be stimulating for your loved one's mind and an activity they will look forward to as the puzzle picture comes together.

OBSERVING REACTIONS

No one ever says anything. They don't have to. You can see it on their faces and in their gaze. When Randy lost all his weight, down to 150 pounds from 260, he was a sight. He looked like a walking skeleton. When he would change his undershirt, his shoulder bones protruded to the point where it looked as though he had no skin. He was all bones. His legs were so thin, I don't know how they held his frame upright. When I looked at him, I just wanted to cry. I wanted to take this pain and suffering away from him any way possible. Your only option is to be strong, have courage, and be patient until their treatment has time to respond to the disease.

Randy is 6'1". He has a kind and outgoing demeanor. He has many friends and acquaintances who are familiar with him due to his employment at a local Christian bookstore. People constantly recognize him when we go out to eat or when we are out shopping. He treats people as if he has known them all his life even though he just met them. He has quite a unique personality.

When Randy was still working, customers would walk into the store with a problem and Randy would solve it. If the customer wanted an Elvis Hymns CD; Randy would start singing in his Elvis voice while he walked to the display to get the CD for them. The customer always laughed, following along behind him. He had other customers who would want an accompaniment song to sing along with in church. These customers didn't have a pianist, so they would buy an accompaniment song on a CD, which had a demo track so they could practice the song. The accompaniment CD would also have three or four instrumental tracks in different keys that they could choose from to fit their voice range for the performance.

Some customers knew exactly what song they were looking for, by a specific artist in a certain key. Then we would get others who may be looking for a Mother's Day song or a funeral song, nothing specific. Randy would always find them the perfect song for the occasion. Not often, but occasionally a customer would come in and tell him they were looking for a song they'd just heard on the radio. They would not know the name of the song but it had Jesus in the title and something about love. They would sing a few stanzas. I would stare at them blankly. I wouldn't even begin to know where to look. Randy could find it in five minutes.

Anytime Randy was away from the store and I was filling in for him (I worked at the same business but at another location), his challenging soundtrack customers would walk through the door, see me, and say, "Where's Randy?" They wouldn't even want to give me their clues to the song. They knew I would never be able to come up with the title. They wanted Randy. He would even make balloon animals for customers with kids. Everyone loved him. Randy had worked at this location for fifteen years, so he knew countless people.

After he became sick and lost so much of his weight, no one recognized him. When we would walk from the parking garage to one of his doctor appointments in town, he would see people he knew from the store and say hello. The people would answer him, but you could tell they had no idea who he was. Randy would whisper to me, "They didn't know me." I already knew this before he told me. I could read their puzzled look.

One thing we did to combat his thinness was to dress him in layers. Randy was always cold, so the layers kept him warm, plus made him appear to have some thickness. The problem was his thin face. You can cover up a thin body, but there is no way to hide a thin face. This is as much a difficult time for your loved one as it is for you. They lose some of their identity. Randy wondered if he could ever get back to who he was before his illness.

It also didn't help the situation that he had to stay out of the sun because of his bone marrow transplant. After a transplant, patients must stay covered. They cannot be in the sun too long and definitely can't burn. Overexposure can trigger GvHD. Randy would always wear a hat to keep his head and neck protected. In the beginning, he wore a floppy fishing hat for months. The hat looked good on him when he first bought it, but when he lost his weight, the hat made him look even thinner. Imagine Gilligan thirty pounds lighter. We finally found him a Tilly hat at a Mackinaw City hat store that looked great on him. When Randy wore the hat, it didn't help with the recognition problem but it was a major confidence booster. The hat looked adventurous and made him feel confident. He could be outside in the sun, yet remain protected. (He now has three Tillys. It's the only brand he will wear).

When Randy's weight began dropping dramatically from his setback with GvHD combined with his inability to tolerate his pain medicines, I knew I still had to keep him nourished. When he struggled with keeping food down, we switched to protein drinks. He is picky about what he eats and drinks, so we had to try several different varieties before he found one where he could tolerate the taste. What we finally ended up doing was taking a breakfast substitution drink which is already full of vitamins, and adding a packet of protein powder. These did help him maintain his weight level until he could get past his relapse. When you hit a brick wall, find another way around. Don't allow small complications to hinder your forward progress. No patient fits into the recovery mold perfectly. Every patient is different, so their care needs to be tailored with their strengths in mind.

Don't get discouraged when you see signs of pity in the eyes of your family and friends at the sight of your loved one. Remember, all conditions are temporary and you will move beyond this difficult time. Remind your loved one who they still are and how much they are loved. Do all you can to better their situation through nutrition, encouragement, compliments, and even new clothing, like a new Tilly hat. You will be surprised how far these little gestures will go to brighten your loved one's outlook.

THE CORNERSTONES

I looked up *cornerstone* in the dictionary. One of the definitions described it as, "An important quality or feature on which a particular thing depends or is based." Your cornerstones are with you and your loved one, day after day, week after week, month after month. They never abandon you. When you become a caregiver, you need to locate your cornerstones as quickly as possible.

First and foremost, Christ is my cornerstone. Without Him in my life, I could not endure the trials I have faced. I know He will never leave me nor forsake me because He has told me so in His Word and I have witnessed His support in my life.

Many prayers were whispered for Randy and me while he went through his transplant. He received cards every day from people with whom he had come in contact with in the store and at church. The cards encouraged him and lifted his spirit. He knew his friends and family at home were praying for him and he was continually in their thoughts. If your loved one is not receiving cards or phone calls of encouragement, see if you can enlist some volunteers.

Many times people are thinking and praying for your loved one, but they get busy with their daily lives and forget to reach out. Print out some cards or pieces of paper with your loved one's address and phone number on them so they can be handed out easily and spur of the moment. Social media is another way to post the address of your loved one along with a medical update and a notice that they would love to receive a card from everyone. Tell all your friends to drop him or her a line. Your loved one will get so many cards, they will not be able to read them all. It will make an enormous difference in a positive direction.

Another cornerstone you will need is one I have touched on already. It's the family and friends who are always there for you. If you do not have these people in your life, find them. They are invaluable. Whether it's a neighbor who can help you with the yard work, or a friend who can help with dinner one night, let your cornerstones be there for you and your loved one.

As I mentioned earlier, this journey would have been much more difficult without Uncle Phil being there whenever we needed him. It would have been tougher without the other Philip going to the hospital with Randy before his transplant and sitting with him while he received his blood transfusions. Tougher without his brother and aunts who called Randy every week, telling him they loved him and were thinking about him. This is just his side of the family and friends. My extended family was equally as important. Our cornerstones are too numerous to list but I am grateful for all of them.

When this ordeal began, Randy and I were both the type of people who liked to handle situations ourselves. Randy is proficient at fixing what's broken and completing his outside yard work. He was usually the person our neighbors and friends would call for assistance. I handled the family finances and the children issues that would arise daily. Both of us helped my elderly parents and my sister with household duties. We were both hands-on individuals, so it took some adjustments on our part to let go and accept help.

Let your cornerstones help you with duties such as taking your loved one to doctor appointments, taking them out for lunch, or sitting with them while they have a medical treatment. These are just a few examples that will give you needed time to run errands so your evening will not be so hectic and will give your loved one a change of personalities they will enjoy. One of our cornerstones would take Randy out and wash our car. Randy wasn't much help in the actual washing of the car, but it got him out of the house, he could wash some areas of the car like he used to do and it took another chore off my list. Randy loved doing this. It made him feel more normal and less sick. He was exhausted when he got home, but it was a good exhausted. It gave him a satisfied feeling. He had accomplished something even though he wasn't back to normal. He could still get projects done. It was great for his morale.

Remember, this situation in which you find yourself will not last forever. When your loved one improves and no longer needs your constant care, try to be someone else's cornerstone. You know first-hand what they're going through and what type of help they require. There are many boulders, bricks, rocks, and pebbles in life, but only a few cornerstones.

A BAND OF BROTHERS

My husband was diagnosed with myelofibrosis, which is 100 percent fatal without a bone marrow/stem cell transplant. From what I have researched on the internet, most patients with this disease are elderly and the disease progresses slowly. Randy was a young forty-eight years old, and his disease was moving quickly. We knew his form of the disease was not the norm. (I'm sure the doctors will tell you it can show itself in many forms, but this is what my research netted.)

Duke's Adult Bone Marrow Clinic was consistently busy with patients. When Randy was living there for his three to four months of clinic visits immediately following his hospital stay, he would receive his treatments in a large, open clinic room. In this room, there was a nurse's station in the middle with several recliners for the patients positioned all around the open area.

Beside these recliners sat a regular chair for the caregiver. As a patient, you would check in and have your blood taken, then go back to the open clinic area and wait for the results. Duke would analyze the bloodwork, and then according to your numbers, they would treat your ailments in clinic. If your hemoglobin was down, you received a transfusion. If your magnesium was down, you got a supplement. They checked nutrition levels, sodium, glucose; you name it, they checked it. This was wonderful because Duke kept a close eye on any possible complications that could creep up. They would catch problems as they were just forming, which would give the patient a huge advantage against whatever the complication turned out to be.

Every day when Randy was at the clinic in the open area, he would talk to whoever (patient and their caregiver) was sitting close to him. He didn't care if he knew them or not. Sometimes he would get up and walk around the room with his Christmas tree (the name the nurses gave the IV stand) to see if he saw anyone he recognized from his previous conversations. There were times when the patients beside us were too sick to talk or just didn't want to talk to anyone, but not often. Usually Randy would take a stab at conversation anyway; it didn't matter how ill they looked. He always felt conversation took his mind off his illness and made him feel better, so it would help others as well. If they didn't feel like talking, Randy would give them an understanding smile, to let them know it was fine, he understood.

In all those months during the hospital stay and clinic visits, we never found one other patient with myelofibrosis. Not one. We met many leukemia patients but no one with myelofibrosis. We longed to have a conversation between battling comrades, soldiers in the trenches together. I looked online to see if there were any discussion boards with Myelofibrosis patients. There were some postings, but nothing resembling Randy's form of the disease. His myelofibrosis was aggressive, the online postings were not. None of them had undergone a bone marrow/stem cell transplant. Most were on a maintenance regimen of various medicines to slow the progress of the disease. It seemed as though he was the only one with this form of myelofibrosis.

While we were at Duke, we would ask about a probable outcome at a certain point in the treatment since the doctors and PAs always told us every case is different. The only prognosis number ever given to us was when we met with the first bone marrow doctor who told us if Randy did not have the transplant, his disease was fatal within five years. With the transplant, he had an 80 percent success rate, depending on complications. Of course, we went with the transplant option.

It is comforting to talk to others who have gone through your same situation and have emerged alive on other side to share their story with you. There were many leukemia patients at Duke who became friends with Randy and me. Some of them survived and some did not. When their outcomes would end tragically, we would reassure ourselves that they didn't have the same disease as Randy so he shouldn't worry. When their outcome would be successful, we would again reassure ourselves that Randy did use the same treatment for his disease so we hoped he will do just as well. But in the back of our mind was that little whisper, "But they don't have the same disease. His outcome could be different." It is a two-edged sword. Both of us tried to make the best of it. We would be encouraged by the successes and dismissed the failures as a different disease. What else could we do? You cling to hope.

Robin Roberts, a cohost on *Good Morning America*, was going through a similar bone marrow/stem cell transplant close to the same time Randy underwent his. On the timeline, Randy was a little bit ahead of her, which was a benefit to him. There were days when she was really struggling, but Randy had already passed that point. He would say to me, "That was me two months ago." He would watch her going through her treatments on television and they were the same exact experience. We could relate to her and her family. They are a close family and we are as well. I would see Robin's sisters with her in the hospital room and I would think, "That was me. That's where I was just a short time ago." We would watch *GMA* every morning, hoping to see a segment on Robin. She is a strong woman who shared her experience to encourage others. It was a much-needed therapy for both of us.

Eventually, when Randy's condition was considerably improved and we were just going back to Duke for follow-ups, we met another couple with a diagnosis of myelofibrosis. After check-in, we'd wait in the front waiting room, listening for Randy's name to be called. We would usually wait in this waiting room for the first thirty minutes, give or take, because the patient needed to have his or her blood drawn at the beginning. Again, we would wait here for the results before heading back to an exam room to see the doctor.

This was Randy's social time. He would cut up with Pearl, the phlebotomist, and Ryan, the check-in receptionist, Lula, the maintenance lady, and Mark the young man who pushes the snack cart. Usually the nurses from clinic, once they hear Randy is in the building, would make their way one at a time, out front where he waited. We'd hug everyone and laugh. I'd watch him talk with all the staff, like a relative coming home for the holidays. Though we were loud, it was a positive commotion.

Looking around the room, we could observe other patients.. Some were just getting started in their treatment, others were in the middle of their transplant, and some were like us, maintaining a well life. If I were at the beginning or perhaps in the middle of my treatment, it would do me good to be in the waiting room with a success story right before my eyes, joking around with the nurses.

After our celebratory homecoming, we'd settle down in our chairs, and sometimes Randy would talk to the people around him while I read. Once he spoke to a gentleman beside him who asked what disease he had and how he had done. Randy gladly gave him the short version and expressed how great Duke had been through his ordeal. He told the gentleman he could not get better care anywhere for a bone marrow transplant.

After that conversation, Randy went up to the counter to talk to Ryan about his motorcycle. A couple who had been sitting behind us had overheard Randy talking about his disease. The wife walked up beside me and told me her husband had myelofibrosis and wondered if she could ask me about it. Fireworks went off in my head. Here was another woman in my situation. She could not help us as far as knowing what was ahead because Randy was further along in his treatment than her husband, but maybe we could help them.

I moved closer to the wife and heard their background story. Her husband was just beginning his treatment. He would be going in the hospital for his thirty-day stay in a couple weeks. Randy walked back to where I had moved and I introduced him to the couple. He sat down and began talking to the gentleman while I talked with his wife. I told her as much as I could about the hospital stay, good and bad. I told her what to watch out for, like washing your hands, wearing a mask, exercising while in the hospital. Things I'm sure the doctors would tell her as well. I also told her other details about where we were staying, how to get her laundry done, and good places close by to get take-out when her husband was sick of the hospital food.

Ten minutes later, the nurse called our name to see the doctor. We quickly exchanged names and I gave my email to the wife. I even gave her my phone number just in case anything drastic came up and she needed to call me. I was so excited to find another couple with similar circumstances. It would have been nice if we could've found someone past our point in the transplant process, but this was fine. We could help them. We would make their journey easier. I imagined all sorts of future scenarios for us. They were a friendly couple; I thought we would stay in contact, but we never heard from them again.

I don't know what happened. I don't know if he had complications and passed away, or if he had no complications and did so great they didn't need any assistance. I don't know. It was bazaar. I thought of all the experiences we had been through, the hospital stay, the clinic, the setback with GvHD, the weight loss, staying out of the sun, the morphine reaction. I would've loved to have had another couple to email when Randy experienced out-of-the-ordinary symptoms. I only know we never heard from them again. Everyone handles a crisis differently. Maybe they didn't want to know what was about to happen after they talked with the doctor. I hope it wasn't anything more serious.

I hope you are fortunate enough to find a kindred soul who is going through this similar situation as you. There were so many times I wished I had a person to email with questions or concerns. One couple we met during Randy's stay in the hospital was incredibly helpful. The husband was having a transplant from an umbilical cord and his disease was different than Randy's, but the process of receiving the transplant was similar. They were going through the transplant process just like us.

We met them when Randy was in the hospital receiving his transplant during his thirty-day-stay. His wife told me the good, the bad, and the ugly. She and I had many discussions in the kitchenette away from our husbands and the other patients. I appreciated her candid words and warnings and took them as gospel. This was her husband's second transplant, so she had been through this entire experience once before. Her experience was invaluable to me, and her husband was a brother-in-arms to mine. This is a friendship that still endures to this day. We love you both, Larry and Brenda.

MAINTAIN YOUR LAUGHTER

L ife is hard. I tell my kids this all the time when they complain. You can wallow in your despair, or you can look at the bright side and move on. Finding humor for our family has never been difficult because Randy is a funny guy. He is definitely the comic among us and many times you never see his wit coming your way. It just appears.

One time we were sitting at the dinner table with the kids, talking and eating popcorn. Randy had something on the end of his nose. I told him he had a little something there (the nice way of saying I think you have the remnants of a booger). He turned his head away from me. I didn't pay attention to him because I figured he was taking care of the situation. He turned back around and said, "Where?" I looked up and he had stuck a large popcorn kernel in his nose. We all almost fell on the floor laughing. He kept it there for about five minutes and asking, "Where is it? Where?" He wouldn't take it out of his nose. The kids grew concerned he'd leave it in his nose too long and he might inhale it, but he kept saying, "I don't know what you're talking about. Where is it?"

It's easier to find the humor when you have a comic in the family, but what if you don't? Or what if your comic is going through a difficult time and can't find the humor? There were times when Randy was too ill to laugh or make jokes. I tried to step in during these times. It was kind of pitiful. I would try to remember funny stories that happened at work so I could tell him when I got home. I would try to engage the kids to share some humorous events that happened at school. When the dogs or our cat, Benji, was doing something odd, I would always point it out to Randy.

Benji used to belong to my sister and was thirteen at the time of Randy's illness. She lived a couple houses down from us in the same neighborhood. My sister is single and has eight dogs and three cats in her house. She has a soft spot in her heart for animals and can't say no when one of them needs a home. She had taken my middle son, Alex, to the pound one day when he was five years old. She told him to pick out a cat that she would keep at her house, but would really belong to him. She did this because she wanted a new cat and of course, she had not checked with me about a cat staying at our house. We had never had a cat in our home, always dogs. I didn't know the first thing about them. Alex picked out Benji because he was so affectionate and named him after himself (Alex's middle name is Benjamin).

One day, many years later, Benji realized he couldn't take it anymore at my sister's house and left. There was too much confusion for the old guy. He had stuck it out for over ten years, but enough was enough. I noticed him walking around our neighborhood for several days, looking unhealthy and thin. While walking our dogs one day, Alex and Rachel both saw Benji and said, "Mom, we need to help him." I told them I wasn't bringing another animal in the house, but we would set out a bowl of milk for him on our front porch. He followed us home because the kids kept talking to him. He drank all the milk. I went and got him more. (He did look thin and it was only this one time).

The next time I went to the grocery store, I picked up a few cans of cat food, just in case Benji showed up again. The kids were thrilled. He was waiting on the front porch when I got home. I told them we were only feeding him outside and not to get excited.

Then the cold weather started moving in. We would put him in the garage, but that was it. We would need to get a litter box and a little bed for him. He would be fine in the garage. It was warmer than outside and he would at least get regular meals. Randy took the kids to the pet store with him to pick out the items. They came home with a new cat bowl, cat treats, cat food (dry and can), cat nip, and a new collar. What was happening? The garage lasted about a week. He was in the house lying in front of the fireplace by the weekend.

The Benji back story tells more of his personality as a cat. He was a survivor. Randy was like me; he had never owned a cat, not even as a boy. When Randy was sick and at his worst, he would sit and sleep in his recliner throughout his day. Benji would always climb up on his lap and stay there with him the entire day. It didn't matter if Randy wanted him there or not, he wanted to be there, so that was that. He was always climbing in boxes and playing with any random items he would find around the house. When he was outside, we had to watch him because he would try to kill birds and chipmunks in the yard. When he would kill a chipmunk and put it on our porch, Randy would say, "This is how he pays his rent for staying at our house. He keeps our yard free of critters." Randy loved him. The sparse chipmunk killings I could live with, but I fed the songbirds. I didn't want him killing them. Randy thought the new addition to our home could do no wrong, no matter what he killed. "He's a cat," he would tell me. "It's what they do." Benji brought our family many days of joy and laughter during Randy's worst times.

Other ideas to locate your laughter could be by watching funny shows on television. In the evenings when the cat was not so entertaining, Randy and I would watch old Johnny Carson DVDs of his best clips. Randy would laugh all evening. The predicaments Johnny would find himself in with some of his guests was hilarious to Randy. The kids and I would be upstairs and we would hear him laughing. Randy's laugh bellows through the house when he thinks something is funny. He bellowed quite a bit when he was watching Johnny.

Maybe television or DVDs are not your cup of tea, so try reading. I love to read. I'm not a big fiction fan unless I'm on vacation, but I love biographies and WORLD WAR II history. I also love books with a lighthearted flair. Nora Ephron, Billy Crystal, and Jerry Seinfeld always make me laugh. I also enjoy books about animals like *Dewey*, the library cat, and *My Dog Marley*. These books take me away from sickness and suffering and give me another perspective. Everyone goes through difficult times, even the funny guys. You are not alone; stand strong and you will make it to sunnier days. Why not take the journey with a smile?

Remember, this chapter is for the caregiver as well as the patient. Caregivers must find the humor in life if they are to help their loved one find it as well. Laughter is a great stress reliever, and it doesn't take much for you to feel the results. Take on your day with a smile.

A NEW PERSPECTIVE

We used to love television shows set in hospitals. Not anymore. We've seen enough hospitals. We used to love television shows with high drama. No more. We've had enough drama for a lifetime. A change occurs when you go through a life or death situation such as a serious illness or serious accident. This change can happen to a person who is ill and to the caregiver. You develop a new perspective.

I am more selective now in how I spend my downtime. I'm done with shows full of arguing. I am not going to spend an hour of my valuable resting time watching people plot against each other and say unwarranted hateful remarks on fake reality TV. I also cannot handle pretend scenarios where people kill, mutilate, or assault one another, all in the name of entertainment.

Life is too short to spend your precious minutes watching mind-numbing garbage. If I sound judgmental, that's not my intention. I do love to watch real-life individuals sitting down to discuss the circumstances of their lives that influenced them to make choices to improve their outlook and lives. It lifts me up when I see someone else who has struggled through something and lived to tell the tale. I usually get another perspective and hopefully I will walk away having learned something.

I noticed Randy has made similar changes. He loves the car shows where they test drive the vehicles, repair old and rusted antiques and of course, the pickers. To this day, he wants nothing to do with any pastime that reminds him of sickness or dying. He had experienced enough pain and suffering in reality.

Benji, our cat who was by then age sixteen, began losing weight. We took him to the veterinarian, who then decided to give him a complete gerontology blood workup. Everything came back normal except his thyroid. The vet gave us pills to give him twice a day. We noticed he was eating more and seemed to be putting on a little weight. We were encouraged.

About three weeks later, we noticed Benji having trouble breathing. He rarely laid down, which is abnormal for him since he would normally sleep twenty hours a day. He would sit outside and stare at a tree while his abdomen pulsed in and out. We noticed this on a Saturday night, so we decided to take him back to the vet on Monday.

I was working, so Randy said he would take Benji. Randy's health was better at this time, but he had to be careful because he would still tire quickly. Since there were plenty of chairs in the waiting room, he decided he could manage the trip to the vet with a ten-pound cat. We were worried about our Benji. We imagined the prognosis would not be good.

I got a phone call at work about an hour later. Benji was past the point of recovery. Randy was close to tears, but did his best to get it under control. Randy had always been the one who could manage the stress of taking our animals to the vet and have them humanely put down when they were suffering beyond the point of recovery. It always made him sad, but he was the strongest one. The rest of us would completely fall apart.

What I didn't realized is Randy had made a connection with this cat who had adopted us. Benji had been with him all day long during his most painful time at home. The dogs were there too, but they were sleeping in their dog beds and doing carefree dog things most of the day. Benji, on the other hand, was on Randy's lap, both of them in the recliner, snuggled in for the duration. Benji knew that was the spot where he was most needed, or perhaps it was the spot where he most wanted to be.

The vet told Randy she could take the fluid out of Benji's lungs, but they would fill up again within two weeks. It was his decision; she would do whatever he wished, but Benji had lived a long life. He was not going to get better and it would be less suffering for him. Randy was not prepared to make this call. He felt the flood of emotion, then the tears. He had made the call before with other animals and had done fine. What was different about this time? His perspective had changed.

Randy eventually made the right decision and brought Benji's body home wrapped in a blanket. We buried him out back under our apple tree. My daughter carved a heart and his name on a stone and placed it on his grave. Tears come to my eyes as I type these words. What's wrong with me? Perhaps my perspective has changed as well.

You can't go through an experience as traumatic as a serious illness and not have your perspective change dramatically. You change the way you view your day ahead by being thankful instead of discouraged. You change the way you view your family and friends; little disagreements now mean nil. You avoid people who bring you down and you embrace people who lift you up.

A five-hour trip to the doctor now means nothing to you because you know it is making a difference. You are able to see the big picture more clearly. You know immediately what is important and what is not. You don't waste your time with what doesn't matter because you can see how life truly is precious.

Now it doesn't matter that your son didn't score a goal in Saturday's soccer game or that your daughter won a participation ribbon in the science fair. Your children and grandchildren are incredibly special in their own unique ways, so don't lose a day not telling them how much they mean to you.

In high school, I observed a basketball game where a girl on the opposing team scored twenty-eight points. She was the most awesome ball player I had ever seen at that age. After the game, her father approached her and told her she could've scored thirty points. He told her to try to do better next game. Even as a high school student, I couldn't believe what I was hearing. I remember thinking how glad I was that he wasn't my dad. It doesn't matter how many points someone scores, "You did great!" should be the first words out of your mouth. Life's too short to let these petty circumstances control how we treat one another. Get a new perspective.

Go for a walk early in the morning when the sun first rises and enjoy the glory that is creation. You may rather sit outside on your porch with your cup of coffee, talking to God about the day before you and listening to the birds sing. Watch the cardinals fly from tree top to lower branch then to the ground and back up again, all the while singing as they go. I recently bought a *Birds of West Virginia* book at a local bookshop and a pair of binoculars to help me identify some of my neighborhood's early morning singers.

If you start out your day in this fashion: coffee or tea, a thankful prayer, observing the beauty that is God's creation, and telling your loved ones how much they are treasured (not necessarily in that order), an amazing day will unfold. You will be so aware of the life around you and a more kind and considerate "you" will emerge. Your priorities will now be aligned because you have a new perspective. Wouldn't it be great if we were born with this new perspective and were able to maintain it throughout our lives? What a different world we would have. But it doesn't work that way. Your new perspective has to be forged.

FIND YOUR SILVER LINING

I love World War II history. I watch every show, read every book, go to every movie, and visit every museum with subject matter on the Second World War. I am amazed how anyone survived during that trying period. What our soldiers withstood was astounding. The freezing cold or humid heat, watching their fellow soldiers dying daily and the terrifying battlefield confrontations. I admire how the citizens at home sacrificed and did without so more materials could be sent overseas. How men and women went to work in the factories to make planes or weapons for the war effort, thus freeing up more young men who would now be able to fight. The most incredible detail for me however, is that anyone survived the World War II prisoner of war camps in the Pacific or the concentration camps in Europe. I do believe it is one of the worst experiences a person could ever have to endure. I watch their stories in awe.

I have a tendency to overdo things when I'm interested in the subject. Randy will walk into our TV room while I'm engrossed in one of my war documentaries, see Hitler or a group of soldiers marching across the screen, and mutter, "Ugh!" before walking out of the room. My kids are well versed in this time period as well. For years, anytime I see a show I believe is exceptional, I run and get one of them to watch with me, and then we talk about it. My kids have even seen the horrible footage of survivors walking around Auschwitz after the Allied soldiers rescued them. (My kids were teenagers; I didn't show this scene to then as young children). This is truly one of the most horrific situations a person could find themselves in through no fault of their own. What is amazing is how some lived to tell their story. One of the best first-hand accounts I've read is *Night* by Elie Wiesel. He survived the horror of the concentration camps to write his remarkable story.

On certain days, I will walk in my kitchen and my kids will complain about how hard it is to be a teenager today. So much homework, ball practice is too long, their friends are hateful, and everyone has a newer phone than them. They know better than to say this around me because if the situation isn't dire, they get my, "You could be living during World War II" response. When I first began using this phrase, I could see the kids pondering my words. They would realize their situation wasn't *that* terrible on the grand scale of things, and maybe they would be able to suffer through their current circumstances. Most of the time, the complaining ended abruptly.

After a couple years, I began to notice my phrase lose its effectiveness. They would reply, "Mom, be serious." *I was serious. If this was World War II, this would be far from one of our problems.* I tried not to use it too often, only when they complained about situations that were really not that bad. I've noticed now that they are all in college, I rarely need my go-to response because they don't complain as much about trivial things. Maybe it's part of growing up. Maybe it's the after effects of their dad's illness. I don't know. I do know they complain a lot less.

You could be living during World War II. When things were really bad with Randy, I thought it often to toughen my resolve. Your go-to phrase can mean many different things at different times, depending on what you know about your subject. Pick a subject of which you already have some knowledge and are passionate about. Choose specifics from that subject that will fit best with your current situation. In my mind, it could be the World War II limits on food and supplies, the cold or hot weather, or the abusive treatment by the enemy.

When I started feeling defeated, I pulled from my World War II knowledge. I took knowing that people have been in worse situations than me or Randy and they survived.

We could survive too. Of course, I never said this phrase to Randy because his health was as close to a concentration camp as you can get. He didn't need me telling him to pull up his bootstraps; he needed me to help him put his boots on. He had many days when he was so sick. I wanted to help him in any way possible and be there with only constant encouragement. I wished I could take on some of the pain and remove it from him but we all know that is not an option. I believe this is a common thought among caregivers during our loved ones most difficult times. You have probably thought the same.

Remember, when your situation is at its worst or when you are exhausted beyond measure, you will persevere. Find the silver lining in your circumstance; there is always one to be found. Focus on how fortunate you are to be there for your loved one. Think about how this situation can bring you closer and reinforce your commitment to one another. If it is not a spouse, but a parent or sibling, it can reinforce trust and create a bond. Your loved one knows when times are most critical, you will be there for them. They can count on you.

All caregiving can be made into learning experiences. It will mold you into the person you are yet to become. Don't get bogged down with the day-to-day drudgery. Find your silver lining or strength from whatever motivates you. We are all different and have different motivations to use as a reality check. Find your inspiration and don't just survive, Thrive!

You will emerge from this situation a stronger, more caring, and empathetic individual.

I LOVE OLD PEOPLE

"I love old people." My husband would say this often when he was working in the bookstore. Frequent shoppers, who were used to Randy's antics, would forget what song they were looking for or what item they were supposed to pick up, then Randy would say, "I love old people." Usually the customers were younger than him, and he always got a laugh.

All kidding aside, I really do love old people. I especially love older women (sorry, guys). Now that I have crossed the fifty-year mark, I am who many consider an older person. *Old* is a relative term. I still love rolling my window down in my Beetle Bug and turning the music up. Old people don't do that.

When I say I love older women, I mean I particularly love women older than me. I love watching them, spending time with them, and especially talking with them; finding out what they were like when they were younger and gleaning any wisdom from their words.

My mother and I talk about my grandmother quite often. We miss her every day, but especially around Thanksgiving and Christmas when she could always be found in a kitchen saying what needed to go in which pot at whatever specific time. Her food was unbelievably good, which I know is common in grandmothers, but hers was *really* good.

Now that both of my maternal grandparents have passed on, sometimes Mom and I will reminisce about Grandma (Grandpa died from pneumonia when I was much younger, so my memory of him is limited.). Mom describes growing up on their fifty-acre farm in a two-story farmhouse that both of my grandparents built themselves.

During this time, Grandpa worked for a gas company to help cover the cost of the building supplies. Mom was too young to remember her parents building her childhood home, but she does remember working the farm with her siblings. I ask her about the Depression and World War II. She said she was too young to remember most of it, but she remembers how her parents couldn't get coffee and sugar at certain times. She said they made do with what goods were available and they never went hungry because they worked their own farm.

They had a garden, several fruit trees, and livestock. Grandpa and their two sons would manage the farm and the animals while Grandma and their three daughters would can, freeze, and cook the food from the garden. Enough food had to be planned and prepared to feed seven people through the long winter months. Food for my grandparents' household was stored in a cellar that remained cool in the summer, yet wouldn't freeze in the winter. They kept their potatoes and canned foods stored on shelves and in bins. When I was a child, Grandma sent me many times to the cellar to get food for our supper. It smelled like the earth when I walked through the doors. I loved it. I'm so glad I have those memories to draw on when I needed strength. Mom told me my grandparents never had an overabundance of any food, yet they always shared with their neighbors, and in return, they would share with them. This didn't surprise me; those were my grandparents.

My mother was the youngest child in her family, so she lived in hand-me-downs her entire childhood, which was normal for younger children in those days. She told me how she always loved Christmas because her dad would get the Sears catalog and order nuts and candy for all of them. Mom said he would save throughout the year so they would have enough money to splurge for these items each Christmas. "We didn't have a lot of things back then," Mom smiles, "but there was a lot of love. We were happy."

When my grandparents were older and all their children were grown with kids of their own, my grandpa was in a car accident while delivering newspapers. As a result, he had his left arm amputated. Mom said when this accident happened, my grandmother jumped into action. She stepped up and helped him with his farm chores until he was well enough to tackle them himself. The livestock eventually proved to be too much for him, and they soon sold all the animals they owned. Grandpa struggled with the loss of his arm, but Grandma kept him focused and wouldn't let him give up.

I love hearing these stories about my grandmother. They encourage me to be strong like her. There were times when Randy was extremely sick and I would pull strength from the memory of my grandmother. I would think to myself, *How would Grandma handle this situation?* It felt as though she was here, beside me, encouraging me to stay resilient.

I watch Oprah's *Master Class* show every time it is on, even the repeats. The show most often lasts an hour and has one person speaking to the camera the entire time with no audience. It mimics a classroom setting with you as the student, listening to a lecture. Older individuals, mostly from the entertainment business, describe to you, the listener, events that molded them into who they are now. This show resonates with me. Many times, I even take notes.

The one guest I most enjoyed on *Master Class* was Maya Angelo. Maya was an author, poet, and civil rights activist. She grew up in the South and was raised by her grandmother. She overcame many obstacles by having older individuals in her life who told her she was someone special. Maya discusses how we should treat each other with respect and kindness, no matter what the circumstances. She also describes how she would ask someone to leave her house if they spoke disrespectfully about anyone. Maya reminds me of my grandmother, who also would not tolerate unkindness, especially from her grandchildren. If Grandma saw you misbehaving, she would give you one of her famous lectures, then throw in a few Bible verses to make sure you knew it wasn't only coming from her but, from God also.

I enjoy spending time with the elderly who do not have patience for those who are unfair and cruel. They will tell you when you step out of line. That's another reason I love them. I keep Maya's *Master Class* episode on my DVR as a never-delete program. I watch it anytime I need a splash of wisdom in strength and love.

I have discussed in earlier chapters how vital my husband's Uncle Phil and his friend Philip were to his recovery. Both of these older gentlemen stepped in as father figures for my husband when he was ill and afterward. I could never have filled this important support role. Randy needed the male comradery. These two gentlemen who helped Randy were polar opposites. One of these men was enormously close to the Lord. He would remind Randy he was young and strong and that God would see him through to another day. He encouraged him every day, and on many occasions, he would pray with him.

The other gentleman was less religious, but he would never abandon Randy. He could physically lift him up when the need arose and would be there to cover Randy if a fight ever broke out. He could even break someone's nose if that need would ever arise. I know this because he has broken noses before. He told me so. He was more like the fellow soldier in the foxhole who would be with you to the end. He was the type of soldier who would fall on an explosive to keep his friend from dying. He is truly this kind of person. Randy needed both of these men to help him not lose hope, just as I needed my mom and my grandmother's memory.

If you have an older family member or friend, seek them out for your loved one or yourself during this challenging time in your life. Ask for their guidance or just talk to them about their past. They will probably enjoy having someone to spend time with, and it will be a great motivator for your loved one. Many times the patient will exert themselves more and try harder for another guy or girl, whichever the case may be. You will gain insight into your situation by learning through the lives of others. If your loved one doesn't have an older friend in their life, say a prayer and be on the lookout. Finding an older companion and encourager will lift the spirits of both individuals involved and will give your loved one renewed strength and insight.

STRETCHING DOLLARS
LIKE TAFFY

I like to eat out on the weekends. Before Randy became sick we both would work all week, and on the weekend we wanted to relax. That meant no cooking. We would begin this ritual on Friday evening and it would continue until Sunday after church. The kids were all home during this time, so it took some compromising about where we would eat, but the only detail Randy and I cared about was that we were eating out of the house. Everything changed when Randy became ill.

Thankfully, we had medical insurance for most of his medical costs and the copay could be spread out over months, but it was all the other expenses that created the immediate burden. While Randy was in the hospital for a month, my mother and I stayed at a hotel about a block away from the hospital. They did have a monthly rate, which helped, but it was still twice the expense of a mortgage payment, plus our food. It took me about three days to settle into a low-cost strategy.

There was nothing I could do about the lodging, but the food was another matter. We had a medium-size fridge in our room, which was terrific. It was larger, not the small type you see in dorm rooms. I went to the local grocery store and bought milk and cereal, along with a bowl and a spoon. I would eat cereal for breakfast each morning. There was a coffee maker in my room with a new coffee packet left each day by housekeeping. I bought half and half cream (some things you don't skimp on) and would fix my own coffee each morning, $1.75 total meal cost.

Duke had a cafeteria on the first floor of the hospital. Their meals were reasonable but added up by the end of the week. That's where I found my homemade yogurt with fruit and granola made fresh each day. The yogurt was very filling and I knew it was healthy. I actually looked forward to this yogurt each day. It was that delicious. That became my daily lunch for a cost of $2.13.

Dinner was more of a problem until about two weeks into Randy's hospital stay. I tried to keep what I spent down to a minimum, but a person can only eat so much fast food. I noticed by this time, Randy wasn't touching his daily dinner hospital meals. Duke had a small food pantry for the patients. It was stocked with canned chicken noodle soup, ice cream, and various ingredients to make protein smoothies. Randy only wanted chicken noodle soup on most days. It's all he could stomach. I began eating his hospital meal, or at least some of it. I always let the nurses know when it was me eating his dinner, not him. I didn't want Randy getting credit for finishing his meal when he was only consuming chicken noodle soup every day. The hospital food was delicious, especially compared to the fast food I had been eating. I would try to get him to take a few bites of his food, but most days he wanted no part of it.

I don't tell you this to come across miserly, because we are not, but we know how to stretch a dollar. We had one child in college at the time with another about to start. Expenses were high and we were down to one paycheck.

If you are experiencing tough financial times, know I have been there. My advice to you is to cut back wherever possible, but keep some splurges (like my coffee cream) to keep from getting too discouraged. I watched a documentary once which involved a dialogue between two people. One person described items he needed to the other person. The other individual pointed out that all of these items were things he wanted, not needed. I didn't take anything away from the entire documentary except for that discussion. When I find myself wanting things I don't really need, I reflect on that conversation. Then I begin to consider all the things I do have, especially the non-material blessings, and how fortunate I am to have them. I thank my Lord every day for providing for us. He's still providing for us today.

FIND A NEW HOBBY

Adding a new interest to your life will most likely bring about positive benefits, both physically and mentally. My grandparents, who I mentioned earlier, were avid gardeners. I remember, as a kid, climbing in the backseat of Mom and Dad's Oldsmobile and traveling about forty-five minutes to their house in the country every Sunday after church.

All my uncles, aunts, and cousins would be there, and Grandma would cook for all of us with the spoils from her garden. Grandpa would sit in his easy chair, watch football or baseball (depending on the season), and chew tobacco. (He worked hard all week. This was his day of rest.)

After lunch, my older sister and I would sit on their porch in Grandma's glider or play with the minnows swimming in their creek just below the house. Through the screen door on the side of the house, I could overhear Mom and my aunts in the kitchen with Grandma laughing while they washed dishes. It is a wonderful memory.

One afternoon it dawned on me that I would like to plant a garden. My family had a farming heritage. It was in my blood. How tough could it be? It would be good exercise to work in the yard. I loved fresh produce. We had a nice, open piece of land beside our house, perfect for a garden. My neighbor had a tiller I could borrow. The gardening pieces fell into place. This would be a great experience.

I decided on an area for my garden, about 20'x 20'. Not too big, but large enough to grow several varieties of vegetables. I tilled the ground, fertilized it, and then decided on my seed selections. I planted two rows of corn, and one row each of cucumbers, tomatoes, carrots, and squash. I planted the seeds and waited with anticipation.

Miraculously, plants began growing. I was so excited. My dad bought me some tomato stakes and helped me tie off the plants. He explained to me, as the cucumbers came in, that I would need to lay down newspapers beneath them to keep them from rotting if they were touching the ground. I had never heard this before. I was now becoming privy to gardening secrets. I went out each evening with my gardening tools and gardening gloves decorated with little red flowers to try to get rid of the pesky weeds. My little patch of dirt looked like a real garden. I was now officially a farmer.

When my garden was approximately three-fourths the way to harvest, I noticed something was eating my vegetables. To my knowledge, we had only chipmunks, birds, and an occasional raccoon, nothing that would do this much damage. I would need to keep a closer watch. The next morning when I took the dogs out really early, I glanced over at my garden to see rabbits everywhere. *When did we get rabbits*? The dogs and I ran them off, but I knew they would be back. My mind went to the most impressionable gardening information source I ever had in my life, the TV show, *Green Acres*. I would need to get a scarecrow.

In my storage closet was hidden one of those decoration scarecrows you buy during the fall to put on your porch or in your front yard. I dug him out, dusted him off, and looked him over. If you looked at him from behind, he could be scary, but only if the moon was out. I still believed he could do the job. I would put him in my garden. The more I examined him, he did appear to be smiling and looked quite friendly, but I justified it anyway in my mind. I'm sure it would work. A scarecrow is a scarecrow to rabbits, right? Wrong! I think the scarecrow made them feel more welcome and wanted them to invite their friends because more rabbits appeared. The following week I noticed huge black crows in the garden. The rabbits were inviting everyone.

Farming was more difficult than I realized. My back hurt from all the stooping, every pair of shoes I owned had dirt on them, and every wild animal in our neighborhood was getting fatter from their nightly dinner in my garden. At least we were getting close to harvest time.

The following week, I watched the weather on TV as I got ready for work. The meteorologist called for high winds with a severe thunderstorm around noon. When you have a garden, you constantly monitor the weather. Will it rain, will it stop raining, will it be humid and hot or pleasant and cool? You go over all the scenarios each day. Weather determined your gardening work schedule. I didn't worry about the high winds; it only registered in my brain that today was a rainy day. No gardening.

When I got home and pulled my car in the driveway, I noticed that all my corn was lying down flat. It had all blown over from the high winds and it did not stand back up. I ran inside and got Randy to come out and look. The stalks were not broken; they had just blown over. We ran around, pulling the stalks upright, but they just fell back over. They would not remain standing on their own. We didn't really know what to do, but we knew we had to get them back upright or all the corn would be ruined. We grabbed a rope out of the garage and got the kids to come out and help. Together, we lifted up all the corn stalks and tied one rope around all of them, binding them to each other. It held. I found out later from another farmer that I had planted the corn too close together. You need to leave room for the wind to blow through. I had no idea. I needed Grandma. She would've never let this happen. There was more to this gardening than just putting seeds in the ground, a little weeding and waiting. Some knowledge and skill is a necessity.

Eventually, we did harvest my garden. I had way too many cucumbers and tomatoes, so we ate those nearly every day, and so did my parents. The corn did eventually stand up on its own, but it looked a little funny after the wind incident. After keeping a close watch on the corn, I decided one day I would pick five ears and boil them for supper. I said nothing to the family that this was the corn from my garden. I had been buying corn on the cob at the grocery store that season before my corn was ready to pick, so Randy and the kids were used to eating it regularly.

Randy took a bite and a face. He didn't realize it but I was observing his first bite closely. He suddenly spit the corn out on his plate and said, "Something's wrong with this corn." The kids picked their corn up and started smelling it. I finally told them it was the corn from my garden and everyone seemed to think this was hilarious. Needless to say, my corn was a wash that season. I guess it never recovered from the collapse during the wind storm. I really don't know what happened. I only know my family never wanted me to grow corn again. They still give me a hard time about my defective crop. That's fine, because we have had many laughs over my gardening antics that year. I'm thinking about attempting a small garden again this year, but without corn. I'm leaving that to the experts.

Randy also picked up a new hobby. He began picking up a guitar we had at the house that no one had touched in years, and he learned a few chords. Before we had children, Randy had mentioned he would love to learn to play the guitar. Anytime we saw a talented guitarist on TV, he'd watch them play. He already had the instrument and some beginner books, but a couple things were different this time. He had the free time and the internet.

He could sit in his easy chair with his iPad and look up free beginner lessons without leaving the living room. It was perfect. It helped him pass his day when he felt like playing and it gave him something to discuss with his friends and even me and the kids when we came home. He would play songs and I would try to guess the title. I could always recognize the song. His skill improved, and I could tell he was more engaged in life. Even when I had no idea what he meant about chords and notes, he was happy so I was happy.

If your loved one has an interest in a musical instrument or any other hobby they have never had time to pursue, suggest they give it a try now. It could be knitting, quilting, a foreign language, crosswords, or the specialized stress-relieving coloring books available now, nothing is off the table. They will only be limited by what they can physically do, which if they are like Randy, could change daily. Some days he could do more than others.

Randy has improved so much that he now plays his guitar with his older friend, Philip (who plays violin), in a little gospel bluegrass band. They travel around to elderly care homes and local benefit and entertain the residents and guests. Randy takes a bar stool with him to rest on if he's having a tiring or difficult day. They don't get paid, but the smiles from the audience are worth it.

I attended one of their concerts at a local care home. A 101-year-old lady listened in the audience. Her name was Mary and she was friendly and outgoing. She had her word search book with her and she would sing along with the band when she recognized a song. The older men and women in the audience will often sing along and make requests. Randy looks forward to playing each Saturday with the guys; it's a highlight of his week. He's able to do this now simply because he picked up a guitar during his illness and started playing.

A hobby will prove therapeutic for you and your loved one's state of mind. It will give both of you something else to focus on besides the illness. Music and gardening were the options we chose, but don't limit yourself or your loved one. With the internet today, the options are limitless. The most importantly aspect is for you to have fun.

ROAD TRIPS

We made so many follow-up appointment trips to Duke Hospital from our home in West Virginia. Many times, when I first woke up in the morning and before my eyes were even open, I'd think, *Where am I?* We still make follow-up trips and probably always will, though not as often. We are down to twice a year now. During the last appointment, the PA said they may move us to annual visits. Duke will most likely always monitor Randy's health, for which we are grateful.

When Randy began feeling a little better and his immune system improved to the point he could get out and about in crowds, we began stopping at tourist locations we had always wanted to visit, either on the way down or after we had arrived there. In the beginning of his illness, his health was too poor, or we were pressed for time so we only passed by many places we wanted to visit. When his health had improved to the point that he could enjoy the outings, we began stopping and taking more time to enjoy life.

On one trip, we stopped at Mt. Pilot in North Carolina. We had driven by this mountain many times during my husband's illness and always said, "One day, we're going to drive up that mountain and take a look." Mt. Pilot was made famous in *The Andy Griffith Show*. The characters in the show often talked about driving to Mt. Pilot. I thought it sounded like they were talking about a town, not a mountain. Well, we stopped at the mountain. I never saw a town. A winding road led us to the top, where we found a place to park and a path leading to the lookout. I wondered whether Randy could make the climb. He told me no problem; he had already climbed it earlier with Uncle Phil. I thought *What if he gets half way up and can't go on. How will I get him down?* I didn't know what kind of trail was in front of us. I can't imagine what Randy may have been thinking his first time up the mountain.

I realized this example was another reason why it's nice to have the help of others. They offer a new perspective and form of motivation. They might even do a better job of helping your loved one out of his or her comfort zone. In my case, an unknown trail may cause "cautious me" to feel unsure of my ability to handle Randy, but Uncle Phil didn't give it a second thought. Uncle Phil's confidence that they could succeed and reach the lookout gave Randy the confidence that he could handle the trail as well.

When we got to the lookout, we found the scenery breathtaking. We could've stayed there for hours. There was another path that branched off further away from the lookout, for more of a challenge. It wound around toward the actual knob at the top of the mountain. This is the site we could always view from a distance, down on the highway, as we drove through. We didn't attempt the additional walking path, but I thought if the kids were with us, they would already be racing to see who could get there first. Randy was right; the trail was not difficult at all. I worried over nothing. My fear of the unknown may have caused both of us to miss what turned out to be a most spectacular day.

Randy's Uncle Phil always practiced this type of therapy when he stayed at Duke with Randy or drove him down for an appointment. They visited sites in Durham such as Duke Gardens, as well as many historical places around the town. Randy would call me in the evening and tell me about his day, and it was obvious the variation in his daily activities was therapeutic for him. I hope Uncle Phil had fun too. Randy acted like they had a terrific time, causing trouble in their unique, fun way.

Maybe you don't have a long-distance drive to see doctors like we did. It doesn't matter. Plan to visit new restaurants or get take-out food from establishments you have never tried. Mix things up. Go to a local park and watch the birds or people milling around. Just drive around town; you never know what you will come across. You don't even need to get out of the car if you or your loved one is not well enough. Just drive to new locations and view God's glorious handiwork in nature. I live in West Virginia so there is beauty all around me. I don't even have to search it out, it's everywhere I look. Every state in our beautiful country has scenic views exclusive to their location. Do some research and go exploring. A shake-up in your routine will refresh both you and the person you care for.

So next doctor appointment, make it an adventure. Find a new location to visit, be it a restaurant, museum or out in the countryside. Get your loved one involved. Let them decide on some destinations and you voice your interests. It doesn't matter where you live, even in the city. Nature surrounds us. I can see God's creative touch, no matter where I go. You will too.

GET TO KNOW YOUR NURSES

This chapter is not intended to undervalue the importance of doctors. Randy would not be alive today without them. They diagnose, plan a treatment, and monitor their patients' progress. In my opinion, doctors save your life and give you another chance at living but it's the irreplaceable nurses that *keep* you alive and encourage you to continue.

When Randy's health took a turn for the worse, it was the nurses at the bone marrow clinic at Duke who whispered encouragement in his ear. They were looking at his blood count numbers that they had previously witnessed on other patient's charts and saw him failing. The doctors prescribed medicines to combat the complications, but it was the nurses who motivated him to stay nourished and gave him techniques on how to exercise when he felt like doing nothing but lying in bed.

At one point, while Randy still suffered from his GvHD and had lost almost a hundred pounds, one of the Duke nurses walked over, leaned down close to his face where no one else could hear, looked him right in the eyes and said, "Randy, I know you don't feel like it, but if you don't get up and walk every day, you will never get back up. Don't sit there. Keep moving." He called me that evening and told me about the conversation. He knew she meant what she said. He saw the concern in her face. It turned him around. This was a caring person who had seen the consequences of immobility many times before. Her words snapped him back into the reality that would not be waiting for him if he didn't get up and start moving.

On one occasion, we were having trouble paying for all the prescriptions. Randy had one prescription that was crazy expensive. It was supposed to support his immune system, which could prevent him from catching a cold while his defenses were down. It cost $1200 per week, but after our insurance paid the deductible, our cost was $265 per week. With all his other prescriptions, we were paying over $500 per week just for the medicine. I told the pharmacy to only give me one week of medicine, and I had them charge it on my credit card. When I came home, I told my parents, who always helped me whenever they could. They had already done so much and were feeling the financial pinch as well. I needed to find another solution.

Previously, I had noticed the advertisements in magazines where drug companies say if you can't afford your prescription, call this number and they may be able to help. We called the number but were told to call another number, then another. We were always told we didn't qualify because Randy's disease was not the specific illness included in the diagnosis group to receive aid. It wasn't leukemia, it wasn't aplastic anemia. It was myelofibrosis (which is a pre-leukemia) with a touch of aplastic anemia. We gave up. Maybe there was a different medicine he could take.

We went back to Duke that same week. We explained to the doctor our financial predicament over the cost of the medicine. We were told there was a less expensive drug, but it was not as effective at preventing an infection. Randy told them to write a prescription for the less effective medicine. He would just stay inside and away from people. We did have the kids running in and out every day, not to mention the animals, which were a worry. We would just be extra careful and keep him isolated.

That same day, while we were in Duke's clinic, one of the nurses who Randy had joked around with for the previous four months, walked up with a little green bag. She sat down beside us and described how she had overheard our earlier conversation with the doctor about Randy's medicines. As she unzipped the bag, she told us the drug rep had left her all these samples the week before. We looked inside the bag.

It was the expensive prescription Randy needed but couldn't afford. She gave us six bottles, which was all that was needed to get us through the remaining time period. The Lord had provided for us again and had used another kind and caring nurse to deliver the gift.

One final story. As we prepared to leave the bone marrow clinic and drive home from Randy's first initial long-term stay at Duke, the PA, who was our main contact at the clinic and while Randy was in the hospital, was getting ready to retire. She had been his liaison throughout his treatment. She had taken the time to get to know Randy well and knew his strengths and weaknesses. She knew he was a picky eater, but she also knew how important it was to keep his nutrition levels high.

As we were leaving to go home, she gave him a big hug, grabbed him by the shoulders, and told him to take care of himself. She then took him over to the supply cabinet to get him a care package. The cabinet was full of Ensure, Boost, and many other nutritional drinks and protein powders. She asked him which ones he liked and loaded him up with a big bag. She gave him a box of masks and a box of gloves to use while he was away from the clinic. Before we left on our journey home, she gave Randy an extra-long hug and squeezed him tight. She then told him to stay on his regime and to get well. She wanted to see him healthy at the next annual bone marrow reunion, which Duke hosts every year. It dawned on me at the time that this reminded me of a similar time I had witnessed with Randy and his mother. As she left our house, she would give Randy an extra-long hug with a tight squeeze many times. Randy's mother had already passed away by this time, so I knew how much this special attention meant to him. The PA didn't have to do any of these things. You could tell she genuinely cared for Randy and wanted him well. She was one of his many caring angels.

Get to know your hospital caregivers. When Randy had a doctor appointment, we would tell the nurses and office staff details about the antics of our kids then ask if they had children. If they had no children, we discussed our pets. Then next time we saw them, we would ask again about their children or animals and they would inquire about ours. We quickly became friends.

As I mentioned earlier, Randy is a unique personality. He truly reminds me of no other person. He is so genuine and he will always put himself out there for you to love. Hiding his true self is not an option for him. During Randy's treatment, he was always nervous when he knew it was time for him for a bone marrow biopsy to check his progress. We were sitting in clinic and Randy knew it was one of those biopsy days. You could tell he was anxious.

Music always took his mind away from whatever was bothering him at the time, so he decided to plug in his earbuds and play the music on his phone during the procedure. The PA doing the biopsy asked what he was playing. He replied, "*Crazy Train* because I feel like I'm on a crazy train." He tried to be funny, and it did get a laugh from everyone in the room. Randy found the song on his phone, unplugged his earbuds and played a portion for her to hear.

The PA was having trouble getting through Randy's bones for a sample. They told him his bones were especially hard, which is normally a good trait to have, but not so much when they are digging for marrow. She said he could play the music aloud if he wished while she went to get another PA to assist her. He decided to let it play.

The first PA returned to the room with a second PA, a male who was a bit younger than Randy. He smiled and immediately recognized *Crazy Train* while Randy lay on his belly on the exam table. He told Randy to let it play while he did the biopsy. I'm sitting in the exam room with *Crazy Train* playing while two PA's are doing a bone marrow biopsy on my husband. I looked around the room with all this commotion going on. It was like a dream. Was I really here, watching all this happen, with Ozzy Osbourne as the soundtrack? It was incredibly surreal. Randy laughed and grimaced at the same time, but the mood was light.

They were still having trouble getting a sample, so Randy turned on *I still Haven't Found What I'm Looking For* by U2. Always the comedian, even during a bone marrow biopsy. The PAs were very accommodating to him and his needs. It will go down in history as a bone marrow biopsy like no other, which I'm sure will be spoken about for years to come.

Follow-up doctor appointments are stressful. You wait for test results and wonder if you will get good news or if your condition changed. Getting to know your caregivers who work at the office, hospital, or clinic will ease some of the anxiety. When you have a more personal relationship with the medical staff, you feel more confident in your care. You feel like you can tell them your worries and fears and then feel confident they will reply with sincere, genuine solutions.

Our heartfelt gratitude goes to some special people at our hospitals and clinics. To Pearl, the blessed and highly favored phlebotomist who never missed a vein. To Ryan, who always checked us in with a personal update about the scooter he rode to work on or his newborn baby. To Mark, who wheeled the snack cart around and gave us a drink and a smile when we needed it most. To Lula, the cleaning lady who thought Randy was so funny and loved to discuss her old family cures for his sore bottom. To little Sue, who stayed after Randy to exercise and keep moving. To Barbara, the local nurse who steered Randy in the best direction for treatment.

There are way too many to list and describe. The list goes on…Angela, Kerry, Charisse, Anne, Mary Beth, Matthew, Catherine, Sue, Susan, and another Sue, Pam, Jennifer, Ann, Paige, Peggy, Brent, Scott, Heather, Robin, Debbie…the list continues. There are many more. Know that you are all greatly appreciated and how important you were to this one man's recovery and countless others, I'm sure.

Caregiver, don't miss the opportunity to get to know those who care for your loved one. Treat them with respect and kindness. They are some of the most special people on this planet.

THE VALUE OF LONG DISTANCE FRIENDS

When Randy and I were first married in 1987, we moved to Chicago. Randy had just secured a job working on the ramp with United Airlines at O'Hare International Airport. It was an exciting time for us. We had new sites to see, such as the Sears Tower (now known as Willis Tower), the Michigan Avenue stores, and the Art Institute of Chicago. There were new foods to experience: Gino's Deep Dish Pizza, Portillo's Hotdogs, and Garrett's Popcorn. We also had new friends to meet…Brian and Sandie.

Brian worked at United with Randy. He started around the same time as Randy, so they were rookies together. Randy came home from work one day and told me he had met a really nice guy on the ramp. He described Brian as someone who wasn't as rough around the edges as most of the other ramp personnel. He didn't immediately make fun of or ridicule a coworker because he was from another part of the country, had a slight southern accent, or didn't know the meaning of some of the ramp lingo. They were both trying to figure out this new job and they had each other's back.

Randy and Brian decided they would introduce their wives to each other on their next day off. Brian had grown up in Chicago so he knew the area. We would go sight-seeing together and then grab a bite to eat. I didn't know many people in Chicago, just some people from my work and I didn't click with any of them. They all seemed too busy in their already-established lives. I was looking forward to the outing. It would be fun to run around with another couple.

When the time came, we decided to meet in a parking lot in the middle, rather than try to find one another's apartment. As Randy and I sat in the parking lot, we saw a white Ford Bronco pull in and Brian and Sandie jumped out. Randy had never met Sandie either, so the introduction was new for both of us. She was all smiles and acted as though she had known us for years. I was relieved. Because we hadn't made many new friends in the big city, Randy and I both wanted the new friendship to work.

After twenty-eight years, the details of that day are a little fuzzy. I remember Randy telling them we were nervous about driving around downtown Chicago and some of the suburbs because we didn't want to end up in Cabrini Green, the housing projects located on the Near North Side of Chicago. We'd often see them on the evening news as some new crime was reported there. These projects were demolished in 2011. At that time Brian said, "I know where they are. Let's go. We'll ride together." We all jumped in his Bronco. In hindsight, this was not the best decision we could have made, but we were twenty-three years old and it's what you do when you're twenty-three. We drove through the neighborhood. Brian told us to not look at anyone and keep our gaze forward. We did as we were told. When we left the area, Randy and I never went back. We never had a reason to.

I also remember telling them we wanted to visit Rush Street. This was the party street where everyone at work went on the weekend. We weren't partiers, but we wanted to see why all the hoopla. We drove slowly down Rush Street while Brian and Sandie pointed out the famous bars and restaurants. They told us which restaurants were featured in different movies. Randy and I were big movie buffs, so we loved seeing the actual places we recognized from different films.

We decided to try one of the restaurants so we would need to find a parking spot. Brian wouldn't park his car in a parking building or on a lot, only at a meter. I thought this was so strange. Brian informed us the car doors would get dinged or scratched in the lots and buildings. It made sense. We just never cared that much for our vehicles. Randy and I always grabbed the easiest parking spot, even if we had to pay a little more. Brian said the meters always opened up; you just had to be patient. He was right; it didn't take him long. We walked Rush Street and looked inside the different windows. We found a restaurant that looked interesting but had a long wait. We didn't stay to eat. It was around two in the afternoon, but it was the weekend and they were already quite busy.

Next, we headed for Garrett's Popcorn. Again, I had overheard some people at work talking about how it was the best popcorn. I remember thinking, "It's popcorn; how great can it be?" Brian dropped us off while he drove around looking for another parking meter. Sandie jumped out with us because we didn't know what we were doing or even what to order. The line was out the door. A homeless man outside the door asked for money, and Randy gave him all his change. He probably should've saved some of it in case Brian needed change for another meter but he didn't. Randy gave him every coin in his pockets. That's the way he is.

Brian caught up with us about ten minutes later, as we were almost inside. The scent of caramel consumed us. I wanted to buy one of everything. Sandie told us which flavor was her favorite, which we purchased, along with a few couple extra bags for later. To this day, it is still the best popcorn, I have ever tasted in my life. (We went back to Chicago ten years later for a gift show and visited Garrett's popcorn again. The same homeless guy still sat next to the door and asked for money. Randy recognized him and reminded me of our earlier encounter. (I had no clue it was the same man but Randy remembered him.)

Our first day out with Brian and Sandie was so much fun. We talked and laughed nonstop. We spent many days off together and experienced many more adventures. Even though Randy and I moved back to West Virginia after one year in Chicago, we have never lost touch with our friends. Our children are close to the same ages, so we often compared notes and pictures. We don't call as often as we should, but we do try to talk at least a couple times a year. And throughout the years we have gone on vacations together. It's like we've never been apart. When you happen upon friends with whom you can pick the friendship back up without missing a beat, those are the friendships that last a lifetime.

When Randy was first diagnosed and we returned to Charleston, I felt like I needed to talk to someone, but not necessarily someone close to home. I felt like I needed the perspective of friends who were not right in the middle of the confusion, but someone who would understand us and our battle ahead. I texted Sandie; was she free to talk? She immediately called me. We talked for an hour. She wrote down Randy's diagnosis so she could look it up. She had never heard of myelofibrosis either. Sandie and I talked and texted throughout the most severe phase of his illness. When I wanted to voice my concerns or celebrate good news, I would tell Sandie. She was always there for me. I knew I could always count on her.

Another long-distance friend who helped me during Randy's most severe period was my childhood friend, Adele (not the singer). We grew up next door to each other. We spent every day together, except when one of us was grounded (which was her most of the time). That's how our parents punished us when we were in trouble; we couldn't hang out with each other. We played basketball, talked about boys, and watched our favorite television shows together. She was always, and still is, my best friend. Her family moved to North Carolina when we were in tenth grade. I was devastated. After she moved away, we stayed in close contact and even stood up in each other's weddings. Adele lived on the outskirts of Winston-Salem, North Carolina. We drove through Winston every time we went to Duke since it was on our route. While Randy was in the hospital for his transplant, Adele and I talked on the phone. She wanted all the details, which I solemnly gave.

Adele and her husband, Mark, drove over one evening to visit Randy while he was in the hospital and to take me out to dinner. It was a much-needed break for me. I could focus on something else for an evening that didn't involve IVs, blood transfusions, and pain.

Don't underestimate the importance of your long-distance friends when going through an extended illness. They can be the support you need, exactly when you require it. Most of the time, a long-distance friend doesn't have the liberty to physically be there to support you or the patient, but they can listen and encourage you through the phone. If you have an illness like Randy's, physical visits had to be limited to protect his immune system. Phone calls worked better for him when he was in the eye of the storm. Don't leave your long-distance friends out of the loop during your time of trial. They may be just the variation of friendship needed to help you withstand the storm.

DON'T LOSE FOCUS

There was a time during Randy's illness when I lost focus. I know the date because I wrote it down as a marker in time when things were going to change for the better. It was April 11, 2013. Randy was in the middle of his GvHD complications and I believed all things were dire. He was rapidly losing weight, his appetite was minimal, and he was in constant pain. It was really bad. Negativity was all around me and I was falling prey. Days turned into weeks, which turned into months. It seemed as though he would never get better. It was so frustrating for me to watch him suffering and witness only miniscule successes from so many attempts to get him better. It was February 2012 when he had his transplant. Here we were in April 2013, and we were still struggling because of the GvHD.

I wrote down the date because I needed a point of reference. I was getting lost in the drudgery of days where there was no positive change or very little. I needed to be able to look at a date in time where things were at their worst. When things were better, I wanted to be able to remember April 11, 2013 and know that we were making progress. I decided to try to shift my focus.

Standing at my bathroom sink, I stared at the date I had written down. I had a little note Rachel had written me in elementary school that read, "I love you mom and dad" in rainbow-colored magic makers. This note hung on my mirror for years. I wrote the date, April 11, 2013, on the bottom of the note. This was my sink, rarely used by anyone else in the house. Only I would know what the date meant and I could look at it each morning as a focal point in time when things had to get better.

I had read a devotional earlier that morning that warned the reader to be careful where they put their focus. After my reading, I darted downstairs to start my day with no reflection. There was much to do before work and I needed to get started. When I arrived home in the afternoon, Randy's condition was mostly unchanged. His situation weighed heavily on me.

After dinner, I paid some bills and made notes on my monthly calendar, which I keep in the kitchen. I looked at the date on my calendar and remembered writing the date upstairs in my bathroom. This is when my devotional kicked in and I got the idea to really commit to changing my focus. It would change today.

I thought back to the many Bible characters from the Old Testament who kept their focus on God. Noah didn't focus on the pouring rain while he was in the ark. God instructed Noah to put in a window looking toward heaven, not on the side, facing the water. His focus should be on the One who would carry him through the trial. Daniel is another great example. While in the lion's den, his focus was not on the lions. He focused on God while the lions ignored him. Finally, I thought of David facing Goliath. Again, he focused on God and believed He would deliver him as he threw his stone. David did not focus on Goliath's large size and his cries of mockery to the Israelites. His focus was on the One who would guide the stone to its intended target.

When you are caught up in circumstances beyond your control, it's easy to lose focus. Focusing on the illness and the suffering only allows it to grow and consume you. It's easy to get caught up in the negative. Whether you are the patient or the caregiver, it's easy to fall prey to the pity. Everyone feels sorry for you; they tell you how sorry they are, "Oh, how do you do it?" they wonder. It's so easy to wallow in the disappointment and negativity. Don't do it! Shift your focus to your heavenly Father who can handle any situation. Hand it over to Him. There is nothing too difficult for Him to carry.

WHEN YOU FEEL LIKE RUNNING AWAY, GET ON A TREADMILL

I don't love to exercise. It's not easy for me now that I'm fifty-two. I was a tomboy growing up and I played every girls' sport my school offered, except cheerleading. It wasn't difficult for me then. Now body parts hurt when I lift them and then they hurt the next day when I'm not lifting them. Even though exercise is not as fun as it used to be for me, I still mentally have the desire to move, especially running.

I think with a little physical effort I could be one of those women who gets up early, puts on her athletic clothes, and takes off outside no matter what the weather. I have the desire to run, but as of yet, I have not acted on that desire. Up to this point, all I have been able to muster is twenty minutes, twice a week, on my tread mill. I know this is not enough. I really should start running. Maybe tomorrow.

When I was in my twenties I had one of the many Jane Fonda VHS workout tapes. The beginner workout was thirty minutes long, and everyone wore leotards. I used this workout tape religiously three to four times a week, although I never moved up to the advanced workout. Who has an hour to exercise? In my thirties, I dropped down to using the beginner workout twice a week, and in my forties, once every two weeks. I never bought a different workout; I liked this one. I did, however, go through many copies of this same title after misplacing it several times.

During my late forties and early fifties VHS tapes disappeared and were replaced by DVDs. My VHS players are gone, but I do still have my VHS Jane Fonda workout tape. I looked online for my version on DVD but it was no longer available. (The ladies in their 1980s workout clothes and long leg warmers might prove to be a little dated.) Ms. Fonda does have newer workout DVDs. She even has one for women my age, but there are a lot of gray-haired women working out on the screen. After deciding I needed to get in shape and stop living in the past, I ordered my new Jane Fonda workout for ladies over fifty (It doesn't say over fifty, but I can tell from the picture that's who it's for).

The following week, I attempted to work out to my new DVD. I really struggled to learn the moves. I was doing some crazy jumping around and my husband came upstairs to see why the second floor was shaking. I can vaguely remember someone calling for mom; they needed me to help them with something and I ended up turning it off fifteen minutes in. I haven't put the disc back in my player. It's not the same without the leg warmers. Now, I walk (with an occasional jog when I feel a burst of energy) on my treadmill twenty minutes, three times a week, and I try to do some of the individual exercises from my ancient Jane Fonda workout so many years ago. After doing the workout for such a long period of time; I've found I can recall it by memory. I don't need to play the VHS tape.

When you feel like running, (and you will feel this way), jump on your treadmill or go for a run outside. Keeping yourself in better shape will help you handle the extra physical demands and constant stress. If you're not able to go for a run, then try walking outside or on the treadmill. If you can't walk twenty minutes, start out with ten; just get going. This chapter is for caregiver and patient. You both need to keep moving.

I also found daily lifting of small, two- to three-pound hand weights can really add to your well-being. I don't do much, just a few different lifts with each arm. The strength in my arms and hands has greatly increased. Now I can even open my own pickle jars. Any exercise you can fit into your schedule will benefit your mind and body.

If your loved one is able to walk with you, work them into your routine. Randy's doctors and nurses wanted him to exercise, but with some restrictions. He could not be in crowds or in the sun. I would have him walk with me in the evenings. When he was first back home from Duke, he would even wear a face mask while we walked to keep whatever was blowing in the wind out of his system. We took no chances. Randy was not able to walk as fast or as far as I could but he did what his strength would allow, and then he stopped. I was glad to have him with me even for part of my walk.

Don't stop exercising even though you have a million reasons why you could. I understand you don't have time and you are too tired. I was too. Make the time and do a small amount of exercise whether you feel like it or not. Try to get your loved one involved. After just a short period of time, you will find both of you look forward to it each day. It is one of the most essential daily tasks you can complete, to keep both of you healthy, in mind, spirit, and body.

LORD, I KNOW YOU'VE GOT US

I hate to fly. I know it's the safest form of travel. I know I will get there in a fraction of the time. I know I will be less exhausted when I arrive. But I still hate to fly. Hopefully, one day I can become one of those strong, confident people who get on an airplane and think nothing of it. I see these individuals on the plane. We are in turbulence, bouncing all over the sky, and they don't even look up from their newspaper. They continue sipping their coffee and munching their peanuts. I'm looking out the window, checking the plane's angle. *Are we pointing down? Are the wings still intact? Did I just see a flash of lightning? Calm down, we appear to be fine.* I'm constantly reminding myself over and over of Psalm 23. The Lord is my Shepherd.

As a child, I was always scared at night. I had no reason to be. No one ever broke into our house. No angry person ever threatened our family. I never witnessed a violent act. We lived in a fairly safe neighborhood. I was just scared. My parents never let me watch anything scary on television because I was always scared—except on New Year's Eve.

My older sister, Diane, and I would stay up late and watch the ball drop in Times Square on TV. We would put on our pajamas, climb on the couch, cover up with a blanket, and watch the old black and white movies, like *Frankenstein* or *The Invisible Man*, which the local television stations would play until the wee hours of the morning. These movies could hardly be called scary compared to modern movies. Sometimes we would even laugh when the monster came out (I would laugh when Diane laughed but it really scared me a little). When the monster appeared on the screen, we would lunge at each other and try to get a scream when the other wasn't paying attention, but I rarely scared Diane.

She always scared me. She was the big sister and she knew how to push my buttons. Even though I was highly restricted from watching any scary shows, I spent many nights in my parents' bed, squeezed right in the middle. My sister was scared of nothing and she thought I was ridiculous. I couldn't help it. I was afraid. Mom told me not to worry about it; she was the youngest in her family and she was always afraid too.

When she told me this it made me feel a little better. It wasn't my fault' it was in my genes.

Eventually, I reached a point during my pre-teen maturity when I realized I had to stop being afraid. I had learned Psalm 23 in Sunday school when I was young, and it had always been a comfort for me. When I was younger, I found the fourth verse especially comforting. "Yea, though I walk through the valley of the shadow of death, I will fear no evil: for thou art with me; thy rod and thy staff they comfort me."

I'll admit, I don't know much about geography, but the valley of the shadow of death is not a place I want to be. It has to be the scariest and worst place on Earth. But this verse tells me even when I walk through the valley of the shadow of death, He is with me. Not only do I have God on my side, he is ready to handle any situation in which I find myself. I didn't need to fear anything or anyone because He is with me. The thought of this psalm got me through many nights growing up, afraid something was in my closet or under my bed.

Now that I'm an adult, I have not stopped leaning on the Twenty-third Psalm when I need reassurance. Every tense situation I find myself in, I immediately go to verse one, "The Lord is my Shepherd; I shall not want." God's got me. Why do I worry? He will take care of me and my loved ones, no matter what happens. He is always with me.

There will be times you will go through situations in which your friends and loved ones cannot help. It is out of their control. It is out of your control. This is the time when it is just you and God. My heart goes out to people who do not have the Lord in their lives during challenging times. We all face difficult situations. Why do people walk through them alone when God is just waiting to be called upon?

Verse two of Psalm 23 reads, "He maketh me to lie down in green pastures: he leadeth me beside the still waters." I have needed these green pastures and still waters many times throughout my life, especially when Randy was sick. How many of us dream of a place with green pastures and still waters where we can retire or have a home. It would be the ideal location. When you have God walking beside you in life, the green pastures and still waters are always there any time you need them, if only you will look and see.

Verse three of Psalm 23 reads, "He restoreth my soul: he leadeth me in the paths of righteousness for his name sake." No matter how beaten down I become, I have this promise that God will restore my soul. There is an ever-present light even when our journey becomes dark. He will guide us through the obscure when we cannot see, onto the correct path. We need only look for His guidance and trust Him.

Verse five reads, "Thou preparest a table before me in the presence of mine enemies: thou anointest my head with oil; my cup runneth over." When you are in the middle of a serious illness, whether you are the patient or the caregiver, it feels as though the enemy is all around you. You hear the adversary marching outside your camp and moving toward you. Now is the time for joy. I know what you are thinking.

Are you crazy? Joy? This verse tells me, even when I am surrounded by the enemy, God has prepared for me, He will bless me and He will give me joy throughout this trial.

Finally, verse six. "Surely goodness and mercy shall follow me all the days of my life: and I will dwell in the house of the Lord forever." I have this promise made to me and every other believer that His goodness and mercy will be with me my entire life. In the end, when our days are done on this earth, we have this promise; we will be with the Lord forever. We will never be alone. We will never be apart from Him. We will never ever be afraid again.

When you are faltering and feel like you can't go on. When you are wondering when you will feel better and the suffering will ever end. When you need comfort and reassurance. When you are afraid. Open your Bible and read Psalm 23. You will find the strength and encouragement to take on your day, week, month, and year. The Lord is your Shepherd; you shall not want.

A NEW NORMAL

Your life as you know it will change. Let me rephrase that. Your life as you knew it *has* changed. The old life is gone. You have a caregiver's life for now, which may not be forever, perhaps only months, a year, or a few years. It's the same for the patient; you will no longer be the individual you were. You are now a survivor. These experiences change us. This absolutely doesn't have to be a bad thing, just different. It's important to not constantly wish for your old, normal life to return. This is your new normal; let's make it the best it can be.

Sickness changes everyone it surrounds, not just the patient. In my case, it had a duel effect by softening me and making me stronger. My softened side realizes the preciousness of life since my husband almost lost his. I'm more thankful when I lie down at night that the Lord has seen me and my family through another day. I hug people tighter and longer (like my mother-in-law did). I try to be kinder and more patient with others. When a person is short-tempered with me, I try to look over the anger because I know, firsthand, there could be circumstances weighing on them that I know nothing about.

My stronger side was called upon when Randy was at his weakest. I drove to Duke each week by myself, rotating with my family. Most of the time when we went anywhere, Randy always took the longest driving shift. Many times he did all the driving. I definitely didn't get in the car by myself and drive for hours alone. That was a new challenge for me. I had to do it. There was no one to go with me. No time to worry what would happen if the car broke down. We had done the maintenance on the vehicle. I would just need to pray, be careful, and drive safely. God and I would handle it together. Today, I don't worry, and if I'm afraid, I ask the Lord to give me strength. Trials really do make you stronger.

Another change I've made since going through this illness with my husband is how I will speak up now rather than watch an injustice happen before my eyes. I speak up in a kind but firm manner, and I always try to give the person committing the injustice an out. It's easier to solve a disagreement between two parties if both sides save face. If the abusive person doesn't see the injustice and reverse their ways, the gloves come off. I don't allow the helpless to be mistreated. We have all seen aggressors take advantage of the meek. Don't turn your head and look the other way. It's normal to not want to get involved, but speak up for those who cannot speak for themselves. Positive change can happen when you have a new normal; it doesn't have to be negative. Start taking a stand and be heard for those less fortunate or those unable to speak up for themselves. Today's the day.

Our children have a new normal as well. There are many jobs their dad used to do that he cannot manage at this point in his recovery. The kids have stepped up beautifully to handle his physical deficiencies. Both boys handled the yard work in the summer and clearing the snow in the winter. Rachel helps Randy every day whenever he needs her. She especially helps by stepping in for me when I'm at work. Everyone is in college now, so they are all young adults. They know what their dad has been through and what is expected of them. I have never heard them complain once. I love my family. I thank God for blessing me with them.

I don't want to give the impression that we conquered all, because we didn't. There were many days filled with complications and the struggles of life. Without the help of others, I would not be where I am today, writing a book to encourage you. I tried many unfamiliar everyday jobs, some I could do and some I couldn't. Sometimes I failed miserably and sometimes I succeeded. What is important is I wasn't afraid to try and I knew my limits. Most tasks that really needed to be done somehow miraculously got done.

Your loved one has a new normal as well. When we were at Duke, the nurses told us this quite often. They didn't want Randy to get discouraged because he was too weak to do tasks he used to do with ease. They encouraged him to keep pushing, but if his progress went to a certain point and stopped, be glad in what he had been able to accomplish. There are many times you have to accept your life has changed. Again, it doesn't have to be a negative change. It can be whatever you make of it.

So don't be afraid to embrace the new normal. Life happens to all of us, every day, that mold us into who we are. This is just a quicker and more drastic shaping of your life. Find joy in whatever you do each day and try to create new experiences for both of you. Bring them a new book, a newspaper from a different part of the country, or rent a movie. Drive to a state park and take a walk, or just sit and watch the wildlife. If your loved one is able, attend a different or familiar sporting event or watch one on television. Don't forget to mix up your life by trying new experiences within your loved one's limits.

Our three young adult children are very different individuals. When they are together, inevitably one of them will bring up some new or past awkward situation the other two were involved in. They laugh at each other, then another one brings up a different scenario to make fun. Don't forget to include your family in embracing your new normal. If you're like our family, you might need to develop some thick skin because new normal or old, there will be laughing at your expense.

Now get out there and find your new normal. Have fun exploring and discovering different places, eating new foods, and learning something new. Live life huge!

EPILOGUE

I hope this book has helped you in your new role, or perhaps your longstanding role, as care giver. If you are the patient, may this book be an encouragement to not surrender yourself to the illness. Don't let the illness define either one of you. You are more than this struggle. Don't let discouragement take over with the repetitiveness of each day.

Find your happiness, caregiver, and help your loved one find theirs. When you feel you need a break, take one. When you need encouragement, call a friend. You are a strong, caring, and compassionate individual. Your loved one is blessed to have you and you are blessed to have them. These circumstances have made you into the wonderful, loving, and caring person you are today. Now go take on your day with a grateful heart and a smile. You are blessed.

For those of you who are not Christians and would like to become one, the path could not be easier. The hard part has already been done by Jesus your Savior who died on the cross for your sins. Simply pray, "Lord, I know I'm a sinner and you died on the cross and rose again in three days to take away those sins. I want to now invite you (Christ) to come into my heart and become my Savior." If you prayed this prayer, you have this moment begun a new life with Christ by your side. Welcome to the family!

Morgan James
Speakers Group

We connect Morgan James published
authors with live and online events
and audiences who will benefit
from their expertise.

Morgan James makes all of our titles available
through the Library for All Charity Organization.

www.LibraryForAll.org